T0132443

I'm Mad as Hell, and I Ain't Gonna Take it Anymore

Fiery Letters to the Editor

Volume 1
2000 – 2008

Wendy Nash

iUniverse, Inc.
New York   Bloomington

iUniverse books may be ordered through booksellers or by contacting:

iUniverse
1663 Liberty Drive
Bloomington, IN 47403
www.iuniverse.com
1-800-Authors (1-800-288-4677)

Because of the dynamic nature of the Internet, any Web addresses or links contained in this book may have changed since publication and may no longer be valid. The views expressed in this work are solely those of the author and do not necessarily reflect the views of the publisher, and the publisher hereby disclaims any responsibility for them.

ISBN: 978-1-4401-5727-1 (sc)
ISBN: 978-1-4401-5725-7 (dj)
ISBN: 978-1-4401-5726-4 (ebook)

Printed in the United States of America

iUniverse rev. date: 08/10/09

This book is dedicated to whatever "entity" out there, through thought, persuaded me to stand up and speak out. So to whomever you are, thank you. My letters would not have been possible without you.

Contents

Preface

Where has Common Sense gone? It sure hasn't made its presence known in Amherst County and many parts of the country for quite a while. Becoming tired of the same old thing going on in the little county where I live, I decided to speak up. Not such a good idea, according to some. With some of my letters not published, and not because they were bad, I question this thing we call "Freedom of Speech."

Some say I should write using so-called "proper English." Well, that is all well and good, but I grew up in the country with "poor folks," in a simple, tough way of life, never forgetting it was not by choice and we had a language all our own.

I do not pretend to know the proper way to write, but what I do write has to sound like me. I need to write using the words that I am comfortable with. I had little help when I was going to school, as most of my kin were uneducated. Most did not even go to school. So I did the best I could. You should write from the heart and that is what I do. This is my book, so I am using my own dictionary, not Webster's. It doesn't make my words any less important.

As the years passed, I became aware that our quiet, little simple life was being destroyed by what some call "progress" and the decisions of a few, but affecting us all. So, I began writing "Letters to the Editor" in the hopes of making people more aware of what we all are losing.

It is very hard when you are up in years, but I thought it was important to state my opinion on many things, hoping I somehow could make a difference. Only time will tell. But one thing for sure as is evident in my letters, people sure will know how I feel.

Common sense had always been a staple in my life and when it comes to my opinions, I do not mince words. Many of my letters are serious, but with a sense of humor, and many will make you think. Along with all the letters of protest, there are some of praise. They are important to keep the balance. Some may even come across as repetitious, but when I ask questions and get no answers, I am like the Energizer Bunny; I just keep on going, going and going. They say laughter is the best medicine, and whatever people may think of my letters, they can deliver a good laugh at times.

My birth certificate says I was born in Lynchburg, Virginia, March 1, 1941. I lived across the river in Madison Heights, also known as "Hogtown" most of my life. It seems there is no other place on earth, because I have seldom been able to leave this county. I spent my summers on my grandfather's farm. Best years of my life, I now know. I married at twenty-four, and have three wonderful children.

I went to Paralegal School in 1993 and obtained a certificate in 1996. Then I applied for a job, but did not have much luck. They may have found it too difficult to teach an old dog new tricks.

Giving up the full time job search right then and there, I enrolled in classes at Sweet Briar College as a part-time Turning Point student; and also began working a part-time job at Walmart in Madison Heights. In 1998, I also enrolled in CVCC in the Photography program and obtained a certificate in Photography in 1999.

In 2001, I was set back with breast cancer, but surgery and chemo were not going to stop me, so I put on my wig and dragged myself to class and work. And if that wasn't bad enough, in 2002, I had open-heart surgery and that cost me another semester at Sweet Briar. But here I am a young 68 with the brain of a 30 year old and it is here I am determined to stay. My children sure wish I would grow up and leave the '70s, but no thanks.

Life's been a struggle, but they say "What don't kill you will make you stronger" and I now stand up and speak out. But that can be a double-edged sword.

I'm into the environment, protection of the forest, global warming and my biggest pet peeves are the government's "over-intrusion" into our lives, and the "over-development" of our rural areas. I will continue to fight the injustices through my Letter's to the Editor, trying to make a difference.

I graduated from Sweet Briar College in May 2008 with a Major in Studio Art and a Minor in Art History, even with a learning disability and it has been a long, tough road. I still work at Walmart part-time and will be taking more classes at Sweet Briar College, for fun, this time. Maybe Creative Writing?

So folks, this is just a part of what I am all about. It would take another book to tell it all!

"I'm not ready to make nice, I'm not ready to back down. I'm still mad as hell and I don't have time to go round and round and round" - *The Dixie Chicks*

Chapter 1

2000

January 17, 2000

Conflict of Interest

I am writing in response to the article in Saturday's (1-15) paper concerning Mr. Bailey and his concern of a possible "conflict of interest."

First, Mr. Bailey, sir, I have found out the hard way, it's who you know and how much money you have that gets you your "fair" day in court in a lot of places. I've lived here all my life and this has happened before and people know it. I've even experienced it first hand, more than once.

In the last year, I've been before the court twice on an estate matter and was ruled against both times. A conflict of interest here too? It's possible, because the judge represented one of the relatives of the other " involved" party when he was a lawyer. That sends up a red flag right there. Isn't it a conflict of interest when the judge knows the other party? And when the other party knows practically every lawyer in Amherst County and Lynchburg, how can you ever feel that you had your "fair" day in court? Decisions are not always based on the facts. And, whom does the judge answer to if he makes a wrong decision? Anybody?

As for this deal with the questions you wanted your lawyer to ask. If a lawyer is representing you, he should do what you want. Your lawyer was not representing the court, or, was he? The quote "my judge" does grab your attention, if in fact those were the words that were used.

Words of advice to everyone; always get a lawyer from out of town that knows no one involved in your case. Then maybe, you will at least have peace of mind that you had your "fair" day in court.

June 19, 2000

The Board and its Priorities

As far as this problem with the Amherst County Board of Supervisors goes, I have the following opinions.

First, it is obvious that the board is thinking only of themselves. Why else would they vote themselves such a salary increase? I think they should get paid "nothing." Serve on a volunteer basis and then we would get the people who really care how they spend the taxpayer's money, because only those who really cared would serve. Just drop the salary and see how many of them stick around.

Second, the same ole group and their "hand picked" people just keep being voted into office. Why is that? After all the years this has been going on, you would think that the voters would get the message. Actually, most of them do, but they just shrug it off and say, "I don't want to get involved," so they are getting exactly what they deserve. If you do not stand up as a group and voice your opinion, how do you expect anything to change? We have a few really concerned people who speak up, but we need the numbers, because the board and most county officials will not listen to just a few.

Third, to obtain change, the taxpayers could revolt. Refuse to pay your taxes. They can't lock up the whole county! And it would certainly change things, because the county would get all this negative publicity and that would not set well with the Board of Supervisors, etc. They certainly don't want anything happening that would shed a disrespectful light on this fine, upstanding county. I hate to inform them, but Amherst County is not "squeaky-clean." Some things have gone on here that has been covered up for years. Just turn over some of the rocks, and see what comes crawling out.

Fourth, the taxpayers had better pray we find more people like Mr. Marks and Mr. Friend. They have already done this county a big favor by standing up and voicing their objections to issues that concern "us all." The least we can do is take up the ball and move forward. If we are lucky, that ball just might roll over some really big toes. Get with it people!

September 9, 2000

Dog Problem

This is in regard to the shooting of the dogs in Amherst County. There was absolutely no excuse for what was done. First, we have a Humane Society for animals that need help. What is it for, just cats? The Animal Warden should have used tranquilizer darts to capture the dogs. If they did not have any, buy some. I'm sure the taxpayers would not object. Then take the dogs to the Humane Society and if they could not be adopted, put them to sleep humanely. The "gunning down" of these dogs was totally unnecessary. On Dixie Airport Road in Madison Heights, some dogs have been running loose for years.

The Animal Warden has been here before and they still run loose. Why weren't they killed? Maybe, because we are not "up in the country" where it is easier to get away with killing them? We also have more kids around here than in the area in which this happened and no one has come around "gunning down" dogs.

Sometimes it may be necessary, but this in not one of those times. Some of the public officials could care less about many decisions they make anymore. The taxpayers in Amherst County wonder why businesses come and go, the shell building is still vacant, and the courts try to auction off family cemeteries with no way to get to them. Simple answer, nobody cares. With things like this going on, no one wants to locate here anymore and who could blame them?

The public officials should be held accountable for their actions. Too many "wrong decisions" are being made in Amherst County, and everyday it just gets worse. Ask anyone who has lived here for 30 years. What happened to these dogs was just another example of "wrong decisions" being made. Someone should be held accountable.

September 15, 2000

Letter to the Editor

I read with interest the story in the September 14 issue of the *Amherst New-Era Progress* and have these comments:

I stress again; the problem here is "the way the dogs were disposed of." What is being said by our "elected" officials is this: It is ok to shoot dogs just because they are "hungry, growling, neglected and have the "potential" to harm someone." Well, homeless people may fit that description too, but I guess they are better because they have two legs. Again, the Humane Society is the answer. It is not the dog's fault they were neglected and the neighbor who fed the dogs on occasion, has never been bitten. As for the tranquilizer darts, the Animal Warden stated in the *Lynchburg News & Advance* "There's nothing on the market that I know of." "And if there was, I would be using it." Well, I know better than that, so I found him some suppliers on the Internet.

You can find anything online. Such as an article published by the Defense Pest Management Information Analysis Center, Walter Reed Army Medical Center, Washington D.C. that is "food for thought." In this case, concerning the shooting of stray cats on U.S. Military Bases. **"There is a greater risk of exposure to zoonotic disease from animal blood or other bodily fluids splattering on control personnel. Carefully weigh and examine all actions before considering this method."** This could also affect kids that may come in contact with the blood while out playing. Think about that! Get the Tranquilizer Dart Guns and give the dogs a chance.

September 21, 2000

The Other Side of the Dog Problem?

It is very important to get both sides of a story. Janet Lewis, who was on the scene when the Humane Society official went up to shoot the dogs, was never interviewed. She has another side to what happened. Her husband told the news reporter that she worked at Wal Mart in Madison Heights and he never went to interview her. She works in Live Pets, which is the fish department and can be paged by anyone working there. She works on Friday, Saturday, Sunday, Monday and Thursday from 9:00-3:00p.m. Tuesday and Wednesday she is usually home. She will be glad to be interviewed at the store or he can set up an appointment to see her at home.

Also, did the reporter ask the vet how they knew these particular dogs were "beyond rehabilitation"? Did they check this out first hand or just repeat what she was told? As for the darts, they do have some for use on dogs.

Remember the Humane Society official said if they were on the market, they would be using them. Now we get the excuse they could be dangerous to personnel, and may take as long as 10 whole minutes to work. Yep, that would be a whole day's work just trying to find those tranquilized dogs! Seriously, do give the person a chance to give her side of the story. She was there and deserves to be heard.

This letter was sent to the 2000 *Amherst New-Era Progress* editor, but the person was never contacted.

September 27, 2000

More on the Dogs

I would like to make the following, hopefully, final points on the articles concerning the shooting of the dogs in Amherst County, in your September 14 & 21 issue of the *Amherst New-Era Progress*.

1. This story has gotten completely off the "real issue," which was the "way" the dogs were killed. A "spin" was put on this story as a scare tactic to shift the focus off the officials who called the shots. But, "if the shoe fits, wear it."

2. These dogs were hungry and neglected I agree, but they were not wild.

3. The Animal Warden said the dogs he shot "were not trying to bother him, he just couldn't catch them." Great way to take care of dogs you can't catch!

4. The dogs were not "left out there." That was their home, even if the owner did not live on the property.

5. The dog in the photo shown barking at the reporter was doing what any dog would do if a stranger were to come on their property. Remember, you were on their turf. There are dogs that lunge at my car window when I go in their driveway, and I do not go off the deep end and call them vicious and wild.

6. In your 9-14 issue, the Animal Warden stated " if darts were on the market, he would be using them." In the 9-21 issue, their "efficiency and accuracy" were questioned. So I guess they were just invented between 9-14 and 9-21?

7. The vet stated darts were not a good idea because they have an

"explosive charge." Pray tell, what does a bullet have? And, you can get darts that will take down a dog, and it won't take 20 minutes.

8. I would like to know who is the authority on wild dogs? Has this vet been here and viewed these dogs first hand or repeated what she has been told? She stated, "these dogs were beyond rehabilitation." How does she know that from a telephone interview? A good home and food has been known to work wonders. Check out the success people have had with "wild" mustangs.

One point needs to be made concerning the Goodman story. The dogs that killed those children were abused and I understand were "fed gunpowder" to make them mean, as they "were raised to be vicious" to protect property. That is a far cry from dogs that were neglected and underfed. These dogs were fed, but I agree, not enough. Now, if the county had given the owner a kennel license, this whole mess probably would have never happened. Clean up the dogs later, put them in a kennel first! I think some regulations need changing. And also, I don't think it would hurt to change some officials. Just be sure they come from "out of state."

October 12, 2000

Who is Wendy Nash?

I have read the letters written by Wendy Nash that have been published in your paper for the past few weeks. After doing so, I find that I have some questions as well.

Who is Wendy Nash? Has she ever been an animal warden? Has she ever been a volunteer in an animal shelter? Is she a veterinarian? Does she work for the health department? Is she a microbiologist? Is she a specialist in chemical immobilization? Has she ever handled an aggressive animal of any kind? Does she own a dog?

How does Wendy Nash help? Does she offer to adopt and rehabilitate feral dogs from the animal shelter? Does she drive around the country to feed and care for homeless strays? Does she contribute to a local or national humane society? Has she ever offered help at all? Who is Wendy Nash?

H. Renee Fry
Madison Heights

October 13, 2000

This is Who I Am

These are the answers to questions requested by Ms. Fry in the October 12 issue of the *Amherst New-Era Progress*.

1. Have I ever been an Animal Warden? No, I do not know the right people to be appointed and I can only lift 20 lbs.

2. Have I ever worked or volunteered in an animal shelter? No, I have no intention of being around any place where animals are put to sleep.

3. Am I a Vet? No, I was never lucky enough to afford veterinary school.

4. Do I work for the Health Department? No, I could not afford medical school either.

5. Am I a microbiologist? No, but I did obtain information from them.

6. Am I a chemical immobilization specialist? No, fortunately I do not like guns of any kind or needles.

7. Have I handled aggressive animals? Yes, but that's the animal warden's job and my taxes help pay his salary.

8. Do I own a dog? No, but I do own cats.

9. Did I offer to adopt a dog? No, because I do not own a farm where they could roam.

10. Do I feed and care for homeless strays? Yes, when they come around

my home, but I think that is what the animal shelter and some of my tax dollars is for.

11. Do I contribute to the Humane Society? Yes, I take care of my cats so they don't wind up there, feed the animals that show up here, from birds to deer, domestic or wild, but I can't afford a $100.00 raffle ticket.

12. Have I offered to help? Not offered, I have helped. By bringing attention to the dogs that were shot, hopefully future animals will be captured more humanly. Most of the time there is more than one answer to a problem and this was one of those times.

Who am I? Among other things, I am almost 60 years old, I work two jobs, I am a sophomore in college, I run a business, I pay my taxes, I am a gardener, and I am a photographer. And, I still take time to bring attention to an important issue such as the dog shooting. I have freedom of speech, which gives me the right to speak out when things can be handled in a better way. And, I plan to keep on doing just that. This is who I am!

December 15, 2000

Trestle

I have been bothered by the continuing deaths of the young people on the railroad trestles. I know there is something that can be done to avoid these tragic events and I have a couple of suggestions.

First, posted signs are not working. Teenagers and some adults as well are simply not going to pay any attention to them. When you are young, you are not afraid of much. The idea I have is to place platforms with a metal railing around them, jutting out far enough to stand on and putting them about 25 feet apart all along the trestle. If you get caught out there, you may be darn close to the train, get scared senseless when the train goes by, but at least you will have a way of surviving. Surely it would be better than jumping off into the river.

Or, place metal ladders that go over the side that they could climb down and hold on to. This would be more dangerous, but still a way of surviving. As for the cost, I am sure there are metal fabricators in the area that could help out on this. I do not know if the railroad would go along with this or not. If they do have laws etc. that will not allow this, I would suggest rewriting them. If they can't, I would get in touch with our congressman and see if something can be done on their end. It is senseless to let these deaths continue to happen when they can be avoided. And to those who say it can't be done, remember, anything can be done if you set your mind to it. Lives are at stake here!

December 15, 2000

Legally Stealing?

I would like to know when "legally stealing" became a part of the so-called "equal justice for all" in Amherst County? There are some important questions that need to be asked about the sale of a historic farm. I would like to know the answers to the questions below:

1. Why would a real estate company go to court and say how much a certain parcel of land would bring at "absolute auction" and then tell other people that it would bring $1,000 an acre less than it's appraised value when it was sold? The property in question has been appraised for $3,000 an acre already. Is that not legally stealing? The owners are entitled to at least its appraised value, except maybe in Amherst County. My 1 1/2 acres (land only) that border this farm is valued at $11,000. Does anyone smell a rat here?

2. Why would a real estate company sell a parcel of land at "absolute auction" that was about to be placed on The Historic Registry and not mention a word about its historic value in the auction ad?

3. Why would anyone allow the sale of a parcel of land without getting the very top dollar they could from it? Could it be that someone has already struck a deal with the real estate company? And if so, would that not be considered "legally stealing" from the owners? You cannot get top dollar for any property without **a** lot of advertising, especially a historic piece. That was not done in this case.

4. Why would anyone with any common sense at all, sell a historic piece of property at absolute auction? There is no guarantee you would get its appraised value and should that not be considered stealing to sell it for less? Land today is more valuable than money. Every year land increased far more in value than interest on money in the bank. Property value goes up, interest rates go down.

5. Why would anyone decide to sell all the "personal property" with the house when it was supposed to be auctioned off the same day on the property in a separate sale? Is someone lazy here? They don't mine taking the money, but they don't want to do the work. The owners are entitled to the best price here also.

6. And why would the court let this property to be sold for nothing? That is what has been said will happen. If the land does not bring its appraised value of $3,000 an acre, and it is still sold, is that not stealing? This county has always had a habit of "running over" people who do not have the resources to fight a battle to the end. But, who you know and money can buy a lot of things in Amherst County. Check out the final price that is paid for this land and who buys it. The advertising of this property has been kept to a minimum for some reason. Wonder what it could be? It is a shame to let things happen like this anywhere.

Chapter 2

2001

January 20, 2001

Real Estate Taxes

With the recent real estate tax increases, I have been thinking about taxes in general and I came up with some "food for thought." Let's take for example, the Circuit Court Clerks Office. That is where all the deeds, court records, etc. are on file. The problem we have here is this. We as taxpayers pay their salary, pay the electricity bill, and the telephone bill. We paid for the building, paid for the furniture, paid for the copy machines, the ink, the paper they use, the computers, and about everything else in there, (I'm not sure about the coffee cups) and we continue to do so. So, I want to know what gives them the right to charge the taxpayer's 50 cents a page for a copy of anything in there, since we already own it all? We are getting charged "twice" here folks and what is that called?

Think about it. This is absurd. Talk about "big government." The county taxpayers should get their copies free. Let them charge those who do not pay taxes in the county for theirs. I have no problem with that. And, do you get help with a smile? No. The only way you are not shunned is if you are a "fat cat." You would think you were a leper. Drop the attitudes. It would be to their advantage to try and be more respectful to those who pay their salaries. This is just the "tip of the iceberg" and if anyone knows of other ways we are getting "taken," let me know and I will address them. I have more questions coming and you can count on that, because my brain is running wide open and it's getting fed more information every day!

February 4, 2001

Letter to the Editor:

I am looking for the answers to the following questions, which will at some time, affect other people down the road?

1. How can a court legally hand down a judgment in a case if there is a "conflict of interest" concerning the judge? When a judge makes a ruling on a case and if he was once the lawyer of a "member of the opposing party," isn't that a conflict of interest? Wouldn't it have been proper for him to remove himself from hearing the case? And, who does he answer too when he is wrong? If you appeal, you go before the same judge. So where does that leave you?

2. Where do you find a good lawyer who will stand up to a judge when he is wrong? No one who knows the judge will do it because they have to appear before him all the time. They can't afford to make him mad. If there are any good lawyers from "anywhere" that have the nerve to put their clients first, I wish they would give me a call. When people are taken advantage of by the court system, there should be someone who would stand up and say how morally wrong it is, even if it is "said to be legal."

3. Why would a court rule against "five" for the benefit of "one" when the facts do not warrant this? Especially when it involves a historic farm that was due to be placed on the Historic Registry. It certainly wasn't because it was best for all concerned. You should not take what belongs to others and sell it from under them for the benefit of one. How can a court even justify that? The court said it "couldn't be divided fairly." That is a bunch of crap. If you have property with various values and five agree to take the property of less value and be satisfied, how can that not be fair?

Court decisions like this will have a devastating effect on others as well, if they aren't very aware of how the courts can make decisions to benefit whom "they choose." They have in their power the right to ruin people's lives because it is "their decision," not because it is the right one. That is very scary. Courts are a joke in some instances. Many are controlled by a chosen "few" that answer to no one but themselves and when they make a wrong decision, they justify it by saying, "the state gave me the right." But unless someone creates publicity about things like this, it will keep on happening again and again.

The really sad thing is no one seems to care until it happens to them. Other people that this has happened to just went quietly into the night. They wouldn't fight back. But, I'm not one of those people. I may not have the money to fight, but I ****(damn) sure have the right to speak out when an injustice has been done, at least until they censor the press. That will come next!

Of course, no response. I am not sure if the newspaper published this one.

March 16, 2001

Shell Building

I have been thinking about some decisions made in Amherst County which have gone unnoticed by some of it's citizens, that need addressing:

1. I would like to know why the shell building on Amelon Road was built for a million dollars more or less and was left with a "gravel" floor in it? Who came up with that brilliant idea? How many taxpayers know that little tidbit of information? And you wonder why it hasn't been rented. Who did they think would rent it? No business would rent it without a concrete floor. Did they think, by chance, the business that rented it would pour the floor? I don't think so.

    Before the shell building was ever built, the county should have informed the taxpayers as to just what was going into the building and what was being left out. And, it should have been published in the *Amherst New-Era Progress*. Some taxpayers can't get to Amherst where all the paper work is kept. Since we are paying for it, then it's the county's responsibility to inform the taxpayer's before they spend our money of these details. That should be done every time they come up with a bright idea. Know all the details before agreeing to let your money be spent, especially in a case like this.

    Think of this, if they had invested the money in a safe account and let it draw interest, can you imagine what the interest would have added up to on a million dollars since the shell building has been sitting there? A lot more than the building would cost today. And, with a concrete floor! Find a tenant, then build. This idea was a total waste of money.

2. I would like to know who decided to "appoint" the county officials? Why shouldn't they be elected like the sheriff and other important people? Could the reason be that they couldn't vote themselves a

pay increase? What have they done to deserve one? Surely the shell building couldn't be used as an example. The taxpayers should elect everyone that handles our money.

March 26, 2001

Bottom Line

I have a few comments to make on the recent publicity about our state government, regarding the local Sheriffs Departments need for an increase in pay etc. This is the bottom line folk's. No need in beating around the bush.

First, the majority of the legislators or (politicians, if you like that word better), do not give a "hoot" about the taxpayers or anyone they have to hand out our money too. The only thing they care about are their pockets they are lining with money they receive from "special interest" groups and their "pet peeves."

The only reason they do anything for anybody is so they will be re-elected. This has been going on for many, many years and will continue to do so, unless the taxpayer's demand they receive nothing more than a salary. Do away with "special interest" and "gifts." See how many will stick around then. As far as their salary goes, cut that in half.

Anyone who is hoping for money from the government, better not hold their breath. It is only going to get worse. We have caring people who would serve if they thought they could make a difference. But, first, we need to get rid of the "power mongers." I like money too, but I will not sell my soul to the devil to get it! Good luck to any organization that needs help, but does not have the influence to buy it.

As for the "dog issue," This could be made very simple. Charge the "irresponsible" dog owners who let their dogs run loose, $500.00 a pop! See how many let them run free then. You could go up to $1,000.00 a pop. That should take care of the problem. And, they could just hand that money over to the Sheriff's Department. I am sure they could use it!

June 5, 2001

Property Rights

Recently I read comments on property rights, which came from an unlikely source. And it is so true. It came from a former Communist Party chairman in the U.S. I never thought I would quote a Communist, but this is important:

Quoted by Communist Party Chief Gus Hall ' ...The battle will be lost, not when freedom of speech is finally taken away, but when Americans become so 'adjusted or conditioned' to getting along with the 'group' that when they finally see the threat, they say, 'I can't afford to be controversial.'

This is exactly what is happening today. Anytime an injustice has been done everyone should stand up and protest. Not only when it involves just you. Some people are afraid to speak their minds and stand up for what is right. "Can't take a chance on losing my piece of the pie," they say. Well I have news for them. By not standing up and protesting you stand to lose much more than the pie! Most people just go on with their lives and not really pay attention to what is happening around them. That's really sad. What is that telling our children? Will they have any rights at all in a few years, if they follow this trend?

"PROPERTY RIGHTS: The right to life is the source of all rights and the right to property is their only implementation. Without property rights, no other rights are possible. Since man has to sustain his life by his own effort, the man who has no right to the product of his effort has no means to sustain his life. The man who produces while others dispose of his product is a slave."

"If some men are entitled by right to the products of the work of others, it means that those others are deprived of rights and condemned to slave labor."

"Any alleged 'right' of one man, which necessitates the violation of the rights of another, is not and cannot be a right."

Quoted from Ayn Rand

Everyone has the right to retain property that was passed down to him or her when left in a will. But, when a court has the power to take that will and because of the wording, rule on it to suit those they choose and not in the best interest of all involved, then something is very wrong with our legal system. We would be much better off to feed the information into a computer and have it decide what is right for all involved. They rely only on the information put in and not who you are and what you have. Humans can be bought, computers can't. Think about that. I know one thing; I would take my chances with the computer!

Rights

I would like to know why the government in a supposedly free country is taking all of our rights away? Let's take for example, zoning. Now, I understand about a community wanting to keep their "image" up when it comes to the type of homes they want in their neighborhood. But, let's say, when a person owns six acres with a 300 ft. driveway back up into the woods, in a relatively undeveloped area, what right should the zoning board have to be able to dictate to you what kind of home you build there, or, anything else for that matter. This zoning crap has gotten way out of hand.

We will take for example, a double-wide. No one would be able to see this home from the road, so where is the problem? How can this be a problem for anyone? If you were planning to place it fronting the road in a "fancy subdivision" I could understand why property owners would object; because you would not want to convey the image that this house would bring down your property values. If the house were to be built there, then you would not be able to get all this money if you were to sell yours, right? According to whom, the zoning board? If someone wanted the house bad enough they would buy it, regardless of where it was located. If not, let them keep moving on. No one promised you a gold mine when you built there. Why is it so important to keep the rich and lower class separated?

We have a lot of nice people who cannot afford a "fancy house." So what does zoning do? They treat them like slaves. Just push them further back into the hills. Get them back far enough and no one will see them. People, according to the Bill of Rights, have the freedom to own land and build what they want. It does not state, "You cannot build a double-wide except where we say." So who gave this board all this power? Not me.

Remember when the blacks were not allowed in the white neighborhoods? Well, this is the same thing. Zoning is discriminating against you because you are not rich enough to build a fine home in certain areas. The local government is not paying for this land and until they do, they should butt out. But, do you think that will happen? Not hardly. There is too much money being passed around. Or maybe we should say "power in the form of money." Why else would they even consider dictating to people what they can do with their own land? There is big money involved here. If you have it, you can buy anything and the "lower class" just gets pushed further back out of sight.

Some people should spend their time minding their own life and not trying to dictate to the rest of us what we can and cannot do with our property. But as long as people sit back and do nothing, things will get worse. What is really bad is that the people who are getting hurt here do not have the money to hire a lawyer or pay off someone. So actually, their boat has already sunk. Lawyers do not work for free and money talks so loud you cannot here above it.

Where does that leave us? Get rid of whoever appoints the zoning board and every other office. The people should elect every person who holds a position in the local government. Not appoint them. That is the problem. Their appointees control people who are appointed. They are supposed to answer to the people and that can only happen if we elect them.

We have rights? What rights? Those are reserved only for the wealthy and slave owners. The government is one of the " wealthy" and definitely "slave owners." We are the "slaves" Think about it. We are forced to pay taxes and if you are forced, then you are a slave. This is not a free option. Slavery is still alive and well, and getting worse each day.

From the "Virginia Declaration of Rights"

Section 2. That all power is vested in, and consequently derived from, the people: that magistrates are their trustees and servants and all times amenable to them.

Section 3. That government is, or ought to be, instituted for the common benefit, protection, and security of the people, nation, or community; of all the various modes and forms of government, that is best which is capable of producing the greatest degree of happiness and safety and is most effectually secured against the danger of maladministration. And that, when any government shall be found inadequate or contrary

to these purposes, a majority of the community has an indubitable, inalienable, and indefeasible right to reform, alter, or abolish it, in such manner as shall be judged most conducive to the public weal.

August 31, 2001

Zoning and Our Rights ...

Some research on zoning is as follows. "Zoning will not protect this county from the Federal or state government's desire for your land, your rights, your money and your property. Nor will it stop development or use of another person's property by themselves as they see fit." "It is not the Right of property which is protected, but the Right to property. Property, as such, has no rights; but individuals - people - have three great Rights, equally sacred from interference: the Right to LIFE; the Right to their LIBERTY; and the Rights to their PROPERTY."

"Where rights secured by the Constitution are involved, there can be no rule making of legislation which would abrogate them." Miranda v. Arizona, 384 U.S. 436, 491.

Zoning statutes violate your Constitutional rights to your property and the unrestricted use thereof. Thomas Jefferson placed great emphasis on the concept of Rights. He said we did not bring the English Common Law, as such, to this continent; we brought the Rights of Man. In a lawful sense, Property is a bundle of Rights, a bundle of Powers, wherein one person possesses these Rights to the exclusion of all others, as these Rights pertain to the possession, occupancy and use of a specific piece of property. In America, "the state" serves and is subservient to The People. We have been told, from childhood, we have unalienable Rights and we do!

Unalienable means – un – lien – able. Unalienable means that they cannot be taken from us, and that we cannot be forced to give them up. Some think it is necessary to force and coerce others to do what a rulebook says is right and proper. They have the crippled idea that men and women are not able to determine the best course for their own lives and must be guided every step of the way so they do not hurt themselves or their neighbors. This is a 'con job', deception and fraud. This is misleading the victims for further plundering of their rights, lives, freedoms and property at a later date. If you allow yourself to be deceived now you will allow yourself to be taken later.

Here is, in effect, is what is being said to you. "**We are going to implement zoning whether you like it or not and with our power you will stand aside as we take your property, your money, your property rights, and your freedoms that you now use as you please. And then when we get around to it, at our convenience and discretion, we will decide how we will allow you to use any of what was once yours and how much we will charge you for the privilege we might grant you.**"[1]

You must get knowledge, you must take an interest, you must assume responsibility, and you must demand respect. If you do not know and protect your rights, you do not have any.

---

1   Fisher, Howard, *et al.* Why Zoning Will Not Work. 1980. 28, Aug.2001.<http://www.svpvril.com/CLZoning.html>

September 7, 2001

Jail

I have been hearing a lot of comments on what is going to happen to the boy who walked out of the Amherst County jail a while back. First off I want to make it perfectly clear that I do not condone what he did in any way, but as far as escaping from jail, the punishment should fit the crime. I have heard of many instances where courts have gone completely overboard on punishment in some instances. I hope this won't be one of those times. Amherst County does not like being made a fool of and the talk I am hearing is that it will be taken out on this kid. I have never set eyes on this boy and I do not know anyone in his family. But the county bears a lot of the responsibility in this kid walking out of jail. Anything man made can be fallible. Especially when the county buys the cheapest materials available. That is the county official's fault. When it comes to jails, you spare no expense, because there is too much at risk.

As for the jail, someone should always check the doors to be sure they are locked every time someone is let out in the exercise yard. I do not care how many lights, bells or whistles are on them. They should also count every head that goes out the door into the yard and recount when they come back in. It should not take a citizen of the county to call out to the jail and say a prisoner is down in Amelon Square. This boy did not leave the door unlocked and he did not break out of jail, he just walked out the door. Also, he is being called a "felon" and has not even been to court. He is a felon only after being convicted of the felony he is being charged with.

The last I heard, escaping from jail with or without violence is considered a Class 6 felony (1-5 years). Walking out the door should not carry a 5-year sentence, especially when the door was not locked. He has already spent almost a year in jail, so he should have already served most of his time before leaving. The court system in the U.S. and those who run them need an upgrade. If they can't get prisoners to court faster, hire more judges and in Amherst County's case, build less "shell buildings" and more courthouses. Or better than that, turn the one the county already has into a courthouse. Of course they will have to put a floor in it first. Get these prisoners through the court system faster. Anything caged up for a year will take off if they get the opportunity. Hopefully, lessons have been learned in this incident and it won't happen in the future. Just be sure this kid is not turned into a scapegoat for the mistakes of someone else. Let the punishment fit the crime.

September 27, 2001

Fireworks Scary

Lynchburg's decision to have fireworks last Friday night at the Jamboree by the James was ill timed and wrong. I live almost six miles north, near Monroe. I could hear the booms and see the white flashes that were so bright you could see the smoke over the tops of the trees at my house. I can only imagine how disturbing it was for some in Lynchburg.

This was terrifying given the recent events. The only way you could tell what was going on was the occasional burst of color that made it above the treetops. It looked like the city was being bombed. I do not think this is any time for fireworks. I know we need to get on with life, but this was a bad decision by the city.

There was nothing to celebrate except maybe for the fact that most of us are still alive, so far. People are frightened enough. I did not sleep well that night. Mental anguish is grounds for a lawsuit.

If there is a next time, please warn people. Our lives have been disrupted enough! I do not believe many are in the mood for fireworks now or in the near future.

October, 2001

Jamboree did Promote Fireworks -Rebuttal

I am a bit taken back by the letter written by Wendy Nash of Madison Heights which appeared Sept. 27 issue regarding the bad decision by the city to have fireworks at the Jamboree by the James. Although I can understand her concern in hearing loud booms, I must debate her statement saying the city should "warn the community next time."

This event was heavily publicized, and stated there would be fireworks. Although an advertisement may not in her opinion be a warning. I do think, aside from knocking on everyone's door individually, the promoters of the show did all they could do to make this public knowledge.

And had she joined the many thousands of people who supported this event, perhaps she would have been there to witness what was initially supposed to be a "jamboree" had all of a sudden been turned into a patriotic salute. I witnessed many an adult and child wiping tears from their eyes as the Star Spangled Banner, God Bless the USA, and many other salutes were played by the bands in attendance.

She further states "there is nothing to celebrate" except that we are alive. What a sad comment. Most of us could celebrate and be thankful for. Don't get me wrong. I too mourn the tragedy of Sept. 11, but if we let our lives come to a complete standstill, the terrorists have accomplished part of their goal. And, for her to mention the word "lawsuit." How naïve.

I applaud the city, WYYD, the many sponsors, and especially the thousands who came out and supported this night of fun for the community. I only hope the one's responsible for this event noticed this support and wish to continue such events in the future.

Scott Thompson
Lynchburg

September 30, 2001

The Points Totally Missed

In the recent letter about the fireworks, the reader seems to have missed the points in my letter. Since I do not find it necessary to use the "Queen's English" all of the time, I may have been misunderstood. The points I was trying to make were these. Taking into consideration the terrorist attacks just 10 days before; the "promoters" should have asked WSET News 13 to remind people that there would be fireworks that evening. This would have prepared the people who do not read "advertising" or the newspaper. The loud booms and flashing light were upsetting to many; just ask the State Police and WSET News 13.

Also, a more important point was this. With flags flying at half-staff, from Sept 11 to Sept 26, I must have misunderstood their meaning. I thought that was a time of "national mourning," not celebrating. "I" had no intention of celebrating anything at that point in time. Wasn't that supposed to be a time for grieving for those who lost their lives? I was more concerned at that time with the deaths of 6,000 people. "I" found it no time to celebrate. But to each his own!

And, if I am naïve using the word "lawsuit," what would a person be called who filed a lawsuit if their "loved one" had died from shock or a heart attack; given the recent events? I like to celebrate and watch fireworks like anyone else, but in "my opinion" the "fireworks" and "celebrating" were ill timed with the nation still in mourning and some of its citizen's frightened. I do have the right to express my opinion and I may be out on a limb all by myself on this, but it isn't the first time and it surely won't be the last!

The *Lynchburg News and Advance* would not publish this letter for whatever reason. I think it was right-on.

October 15, 2001

Festival Sends Mixed Message

It has been brought to my attention by a festival attendee that a mixed message is being sent by the Garlic Festival. First, the festival itself is great, but the intoxication by a great many of the attendees is not. What you have here is the following. You put on a Garlic Festival, which brings out a lot of people. Then you add the wine and you have a flood of people. The problem is this, you have a great many people "under the influence," with wine glasses hanging around their necks and wine bottles in their hands. They are throwing up everywhere, lying around on blankets with wine bottles thrown all over the vineyard. It is ok to have fun but when you are allowed to get in your car and drive under the influence, when it is illegal that sends a mixed message.

There is no way every drinker had a designated driver and when you drink until you leave, you cannot possibly leave sober. The deputies are there, but to do their job, they would have to ticket everyone and there are just not enough deputies to follow every intoxicated driver. Singling out a few does not solve the problem.

This problem is not the fault of the Sheriff's Department, but it is the fault of whoever permits this to go on. Would the county hire enough deputies to write all those tickets? No way. It seems the bottom line is this. People are allowed to "drink and drive" because it brings a lot of money into the county and some in an "important position" allowed this to go on. So, the county should provide transportation to those in attendance so the roads will be safe. With the people that stay during the festival, the county makes just as much money as the festival. There is nothing wrong with having festivals, but someone should look out for the sober people on the roads, when there is drinking involved to the degree it is. Next year, go to the festival and see for yourself.

October 22, 2001

Board of Waste

Mr. Marks was right on the money in his letter about the Brockman Industrial Park. Since we already have one empty Industrial Park lets "do" build another and go deeper into the hole. The Board is not "supervising" anything according to many, unless its "waste." The taxpayers in the county had better stand up and voice their objections about the things the Board of Supervisors are wasting our hard earned tax dollars on. The hole is going to be so deep before long, our great, great, grandchildren will not be able to crawl out of it. If the county wants to give away our money, put it to "good" use.

Hire enough deputies to ticket "all" of the drivers "under the influence" leaving the Garlic Festival. That would generate enough money to pay the whole county out of debt. Amherst is the only county I know of that allows a flood of drivers "under the influence" on the road when it means "dollars." And that is not the Sheriff's Departments fault. It rests squarely on the shoulders of the people who okayed the serving of alcohol to that many people two days running from beginning to end. I understand that message to say, "laws can be broken and people can be put in jeopardy, as long as we bring in thousands of people and we get the money; and they do in the form of a variety of taxes.

Also, I have a suggestion to make on how we can keep an eye on our money. Place the accounting records of the money they take in and all the expenses they pay out, to whom and for what, on the county web site where the taxpayers can have access to it "anytime." We have that right, because it is our money. Just have the taxpayers use a password to access them. And, I will go one better, if they scream, they can't afford it, I will go out there and do it for them for "free. Now that is a deal they can't pass up, unless? People, stand up and speak out on how your tax dollars are being spent. Remember the majority rules.

Chapter 3

2002

January 10, 2002

Change Needed

I would like to know why the Counsel for Amherst County would send $107,778.65 of other people's inheritance money through the mail uninsured? Now, you know those lawyer's knew better than that. Who would replace it if it were stolen, the law firm or the Amherst County taxpayers? Can you see them paying that much money out of our tax dollars? Is that why it wasn't insured?

Because then, someone out in Amherst would have to pay it back. This borders on incompetence. It should have been hand delivered to the person responsible for paying it out.

What is this saying about the "officials" out in Amherst who retained this firm to be Counsel for Amherst County? And they are supposed to be making good decisions as to how to best handle our tax dollars? Give me a break. I could have done better with no brain. It is getting to the point that we need a complete job of " cleaning house" in Amherst and start over with people who do not control every person they appoint. The "old guard" has ruled long enough.

And as long as they keep putting " their" hand picked people in office, things are going to get worse. We voted them into office and we can vote them out. Follow Martinsville's lead. If they won't go, circulate petitions and have them removed. We deserve better than what we have now and one good example is to check out your new tax assessments. Now what do you think that extra money is going for? New schools? Nope, the Brockman Industrial Park most likely and a pay raise for them. If you really want more money fellows, pay yourselves nothing. With the decisions you have been making lately, that is exactly what most of you deserve. And that goes for your counsel too.

February 8, 2002

Budget

In regard to the proposed future budget, I have some concerns. First, the $3.16 million they want for the landfill from 2002-2004 is for what improvements? If I remember correctly, it's practically new. Why does it need improvements? Is it because it wasn't done right in the first place, or are they planning on hauling in New Jersey, New York's, etc. garbage and dump it here for the money; and need more room? It has happened in other parts of the state.

Second, they want $500,000 for a new communications center, and $500,000 for a new rescue and fire training center in 2005-2006. Not with the shape the economy is in! They can kill two birds with one stone here. Put both in the shell building we already have on Amelon Road. I am sure the computers that handle the 911 calls do not care where they will be placed. They do not take up $500,000 worth of room. It's people who want the luxury accommodations, not the computers. Waste of taxpayer's dollars!

Third, we do not desperately need a new $2.25 million rescue and fire station in 2004-2005. They are doing ok in the buildings they are located in now. Fix them up if necessary. They have been managing ok up to this point. The people who are making these elaborate decisions need to tighten up. We do not have the tax dollars for these "state of the art" buildings now, unless they raise the real estate taxes again.

Fourth, what kind of fools would spend $1.5 million dollars on a fishing pier and suspended bridge? Is this bridge crossing an ocean? A drastic waste of taxpayer's dollars! If people want to get to the other side, paddle a canoe. I sure would before I would agree to spend this kind of money for a bridge. With the economy in recession, it's just plain stupid to spend tax dollars on anything that is not urgently needed right now or in the near future. Remember that when 2004-2006 gets here, this projected budget will most likely be five times larger than it is now. We can't afford it today, so you can imagine what it will cost us then. If you think real estate taxes are bad now, just wait a few years.

People are tired of their hard earned tax dollars being squandered. We need people with common sense to make the decisions about how our tax dollars are being spent and not what appear to be educated fools. Pass the word, it's time to come together and discuss what our options are. And we do have some.

February 23, 2002

Water Hook Up

As luck would have it, another problem for us taxpayers. It has to do with an article in the *Lynchburg News & Advance* on the Board's latest decision to control our lives as well as our money. Preston Bryant, R-Lynchburg has introduced Bill 1130 in the Senate that would "allow the taxpayers of undeveloped land the ability to use private water and sewer systems, even if the county has a mandatory hookup policy."

And as usual the Board is determined to see that doesn't happen. They have drafted a letter to Frank Ruff, R-Mecklenburg County and Steve Newman, R-Lynchburg asking them to oppose this bill. They say they are concerned about "creating long-term environmental problems." Now this is where "common sense" comes into play. We have had wells and septic tanks around for way over 60 years and I have not heard of any that have created any environmental problems. They also say the bill would hinder the county's growth. How? By not being able to rob us blind? They are the ones who are hindering growth and in "royal fashion."

This is just another way to control our lives even more. They are trampling on our rights when they try to "force us" to use county hookups. The Bill of Rights does not give them that power. If they get by with this, what's next? Everyone must write, e-mail or phone your representatives and demand they support this bill. Remind them another election is coming up. Contact Del. Preston Bryant and thank him for trying to look out for us. He is the kind of representative we need. Our rights are in jeopardy here and it's only the beginning. If we do not speak up now, all of our rights will be gone a lot sooner they you think. Contact those representatives now. It doesn't hurt to try to make a difference, but it sure will hurt if we do nothing. And the way things are going; pray we still have a voice when the next election comes around.

March 31, 2002

Tax Raise

Well, the "tax raise" is upon us again. I read with interest the article about another tax increase in the March 28, issue of *The Amherst New-Era Progress*. It stated, "Services cost money." Well, we already know that. You also said the taxpayers expected them. I beg to differ from you on that issue. Just pole the taxpayers and see for yourself. The problem here is the taxpayers were not asked if we wanted to provide those services. There is no way one Supervisor can speak for all of the taxpayers in his district. Let the taxpayers vote on each service as to whether they want it or not.

If we decide we want the service, then the board can pay it out of our tax dollars. Not before. This spending crap has gotten way out of hand. The Board should be aware; people are getting fed up. We control our tax dollars.

Now, I have a suggestion as to how the county can accumulate a lot of money with no effort whatsoever. Why raise every tax in sight when you can have money come from the court right into your greedy "big" hands. Just triple the fines and court cost. That should wake up a few violators. Add up the fines and court cost on a given day, triple that and sees what you come up with, a tremendous amount of money.

Take for example the judgments for March 19, which totaled $ 3,254.00 and that was only the one's that had their fines listed. Triple that and you have $9,760.00. And that was just for one day. The court can take their $30.00 per fine and the rest can be paid out for "necessary services," starting with fixing our potholes, etc. Make those who break the law pay through the nose and give us hard working taxpayers a break. We are tired of it, boys. Just wait until the next election. We will put an ordinary working man next door in your office and you will see some common sense used then. Sometimes having too many smarts can work against you!

The court costs have disappeared from the newspaper. I wonder why? Why hide the fines they take in????

May 6, 2002

To the Officials of Amherst County:

I would just like to say it is about time some of you guy's made a decision that we can be proud of. That decision was to name Ernie Guill principal of Amherst County High School. What I would like to know is "why" it took you 30 + years to do it? Up to now every principal that was brought in turned around and left. Could it have been because you were telling them how to do their job? If Mr. Guill had been placed in that position from the beginning, you would have seen a vast improvement in Amherst County High a long time ago.

Both the students and teachers alike respect him. There is no one that "could have" or "can" do a better job as principal. And I would like to offer one word of advice. Do not try to control him like so many other people are controlled in this county. Leave the man alone and let him do "his" job "his" way.

A man with his experience does not need anyone telling him how to run a high school. I know it will be very difficult to reframe from letting someone else have a say in the decisions that you have been making for all of these years, but do try. Listen to what he has to say and support him. 30+ years at Amherst County High gives him that right. The whole county will benefit from it if you do.

May 13, 2002

Junk Cars

I would like to thank Mr. Albert and Mr. Fore for voting against the proposed ordinance giving the county the authority to remove junk cars. Now don't get me wrong for a minute. I would not like a bunch of junk cars next to me either. But there is a much more important issue here than whether I like it or not. And that is the rights given "all of us" by the Constitution. If my neighbor has junk cars and I don't like it, well to bad for me. He has that right. And if others or I cannot work it out with our neighbor, just put up a wall or move. It may be a little inconvenient, but not nearly as inconvenient as when all our rights are gone by letting the "local government" take anything we own just because they can vote themselves that power.

The government overstepped its bounds long ago when it comes to stepping on our rights. No one should have the power to dictate to people what he or she "cannot" have on their property. As of today we do not live in a Communist country, but that is changing fast and it will happen if "all taxpayers" do not stand up and voice their opinion on their rights. What are we afraid of? There are more taxpayers than "officials" And the jail won't hold us all. It is nothing wrong about "peaceful protest." In my opinion it is way overdue. The taxpayers have put the board on notice. We will remember come election day.

May 30, 2002

An Unsightly View to All?

In regard to the zoning ordinance that is trying to be passed, the following should be said. Who has been given the power (by God or the taxpayers) to determine what is or is not an "unsightly view"? The "unsightly view" that is being talked about has been in the county for many, many years. Remember, we are living in Amherst County and not in Hollywood.

A "few" cars in a yard here are a way of life, especially on side roads. Now in subdivisions, do what you want. Set up your own rules. But, the rest of us "simple living" people want to be left alone. This is a way of life for many and if you do not want to have an "unsightly view," be careful where you build or buy. Those who wish to move here should check out the neighborhood and if it doesn't suit you, move on, but do not try to push your views of what is "unsightly" down the throats of the other taxpayers. The whole county does not look alike and it should stay that way. We are a diverse group here in Amherst County. The "government" does not have a duty to help us to protect our investments and our way of life around us, unless they protect us "all" and that includes the "simple living" people, not just the people who have money.

It seems the government can't keep it's own house in order, let alone it's citizens. Look at the mess we are in and decide for yourselves. Amherst County does not need to be an "image builder" at the expense of the rights of our "simple living" people. If you do not want to live in Amherst County with it's diverse people and culture, move to Lynchburg. Our taxes will all be the same soon! What is an "eye-sore" to some is a way of life to others. We have our rights too.

June 22, 2002

Candidates Forum Needed

Before the next local election, the taxpayers need to come together and demand a Candidates Forum. We need to get an idea as to where those who are running stand on issues that involve our rights and tax dollars. Lynchburg has forum's where the candidates answer questions from the taxpayers and Amherst County should have it too. That is the only way we will get any idea as to whom we are electing. I also urge *The Amherst New-Era-Progress* to publish the voting records on the Board of Supervisors as to how they voted on issues that affected us taxpayers. It sure isn't on the web site. The last time I tried to go there, the web site was gone! How convenient for them.

The only way we can protect the rights we still have is to be sure of whom we put in office. I am sick and tired of losing my rights and I plan to get the ones I have already lost back, if I have to go to every People's Rights Groups in America. Maybe some national publicity will get their attention.

The Constitution does not give the government the power to take what we bought and paid for or control what we do with it. They say they are doing this for the good of the people, but they are doing it because of money and they are ruining us in the process. They are just like the "big boys," pressured by special interest. They need to distance themselves from the "power mongers" and take a long hard look at what they are doing to the people's rights. Most could care less about the taxpayers. It's "gimme the money." But, we have many taxpayers that put "rights" above money. These are the ones we need to put in office. Urge them to run. The time to start is now. We must be prepared for the next election.

July 27, 2002

Adult Entertainment

Just when you think things cannot get any worse in Amherst County; here comes the idea of allowing adult entertainment in. Now, this idea is a new low by the county officials to obtain money. We have drug dealers, bookmakers and crooks already here. That is enough corruption. We do not need adult entertainment. After all, it's free on the Internet.

But no, this is just another scheme to obtain money and use the First Amendment as an excuse. I can just imagine how a meeting would go: "*Let's see boy's, are we making money on adult bookstores? No, they are in Lynchburg. Okay, are we making money on adult movie? No, they are in Lynchburg. Well, maybe we are making money on strip clubs? No, they are in Roanoke. Gee fellows, we have a problem here. We need our own adult entertainment right here in the county. After all, the taxpayers have let us get away with everything else. Why not this? This should be a piece of cake. We'll just blame the First Amendment.*"

What they would be saying here is anything goes if it produces money. It's not the county's fault it cannot attract favorable businesses, it's the officials who messed things up. Bad decisions over the years are the real reason things have hit rock bottom and not the lack of money. As for adult entertainment, we do not need that trash in the county. The officials here do not speak for all of the taxpayers. That's impossible. Many cannot get out to the meetings, so send out letters to all the taxpayers and let them decide or put it on the ballot, boys! No, they would not allow that to happen. But wait; there is a glimmer of light on the horizon. Let's elect new officials. Ones who will let the taxpayers decide what we will or will not allow in our county. We have the power to stop this in its tracks. Adult entertainment in the county? When pigs fly!

August 5, 2002

Do As I Say, Not As I Do?

There seems to be a "double standard" going on in Amherst County. The county ordinance says you cannot put certain things on your property because it is unsightly or it harms the environment. If you disobey you will be fined or thrown in jail. So, how can officials in Amherst County get by with letting a dumpsite be created and hid it? Or so they think. Who do they think they are? We have to live by the ordinances and they don't? They need to pass an ordinance to protect us from them. What I am referring to is the new 130 Connector that is passing through the Mantiply Farm property. One part has become a dumpsite. The state is doing the dumping, but it has to be with the blessing of Amherst County officials. Nothing goes on without their knowledge.

They are digging holes the depth of a two-story building and filling them with rock, metal, anything that will not burn and concrete chunks that look like pillars from under the World Trade Center. It is a clear case of environmental pollution. This will damage the environment far worse than a car sitting above ground. One day the land will wind up in someone else's hands and if they want to build there, they are out of luck. No septic or basement on that piece of property. That part of the land has become worthless.

This property should be flagged in the deed books as a dumpsite so those future potential owners will be aware of what they are buying. This is happening simply because someone is too cheap to haul it to a proper dumpsite? Another bad decision! And, a warning to individuals or businesses that are considering buying land in Amherst County. Don't buy anything that is not a forest. You could very possibly be buying a dumpsite.

September 20, 2002

Polluted Water?

As if things are not bad enough, now we are drinking polluted water. With some people, this may take a long time to affect their health, but with people who have already had cancer, this is very dangerous. Do you sue if you suddenly have it reoccur? You can if you link it to the water. And they have already stated it could cause cancer. Now that we know the water is polluted; the question is how long will it take it to kill us? How did the water get to this point? Someone was not doing his or her job? Why did they let it get so far above the standard before warning people? Our water did not violate water standards, the water officials did. Did they get caught? Is that the reason they informed the taxpayers? How do we know that this hasn't been going on for years?

Now according to them it will fix itself when the weather changes in 2003. That is too long to wait. Some of us may be dead by then. If the county plans to continue to sell us polluted water, which violates the water standards, isn't that illegal? What price do they pay? You should not be allowed to "give away" polluted water. They should be made to provide safe water to us. That is what we pay for.

The whole state is in the same boat here, and I haven't heard of their water being polluted. Something smells here and it sure ain't the fish. If anybody buys bottled water, the county should pay for it. That is where the ball stops. They are the ones who were supposed to be safeguarding our water supply. At least that's what I thought we were paying them for. And, as for our "understanding." Poppycock. Not when I am paying for polluted water that will affect my health. If you are interested in bottled water, Wal-Mart has plenty and it is cheaper than this pollution the county is peddling. Buy it, put your receipt in an envelope, mail it to Amherst and demand a refund.

September 20, 2002

Dangerous Road

Someone in the business of making decisions in Amherst have their priorities wrong when it comes to making decisions on what roads that need to be widened and/or paved. Here it is in a nutshell. We have Dixie Airport Road, which has been widened and paved, is nice and smooth and a joy to drive on. It supports quite a few subdivisions and it has a lot of cars, which would account for it's being so well maintained. The speed limit is 35 mph.

Then we have Coolwell Road, which also has quite a few subdivisions and it also has a lot of traffic. It is nice and wide and the north end had just been paved and is also a joy to drive on. But, then we have Izaak Walton Road. Now I ask you this. The road has quite a few subdivisions, a sawmill off of it and the best of all, the county dump. Now, why is this road which is no wider than a pig path and drives like you are running over a washboard, knocking your front end out of line, and gigantic garbage trucks which hog the road and fly like bats out of hell, support a speed limit of 45 mph?

Something is very wrong here. This road is dangerous and will it take someone getting killed by a garbage truck to light a fire under the officials? How can anyone justify 45 mph on a pig path and only 35 mph on nice wide roads? And it is not a matter of money. We pay hard earned tax dollars to maintain the roads and the people on Izaak Walton Road deserve a road as safe as the other two mentioned. If the county cannot take care of this problem pronto, before somebody dies from these "trucks from hell," then the taxpayers will have to keep some of their tax dollars and fix it themselves.

October 20, 2002

Pedlar Reservoir

I would like to know the answers to the following question: I understand Lynchburg built the Pedlar Reservoir. Is this not in Amherst County? Did they sell the land to Lynchburg or does the county still own it? If we own it, why did we not build it and have plenty of water? I do not know what kind of deal they struck with Lynchburg, but we should find out. If we own the land, we have a right to half of the water. Is it the dollar talking again?

As for the county saving money, a concerned taxpayer suggested the county cut out all of the "free rides." Those are the cars we provide the officials with to ride around the state in. Since times are tight, drive your own car, like the rest of us (with the exception of law enforcement of course). It's a waste of our money. Salary is one thing, but fringe benefits are something else, of which I did not agree to provide.

From a song by Don Henley: "While you were sleeping, they came and took it away, the lanes and the meadows, the places you use to play. It was an inside job by the well connected, your little protest summarily rejected".

We need to start a web page for the taxpayers to ask questions, make suggestions and vent their frustrations. If anyone could help set it up please do. It could benefit us all.

November 10, 2002

Mailboxes

I have heard that nothing was suppose to be put in the mailbox except mail, and I just brushed it off as "no big deal." I never thought much about it until I found my newspaper strode all over the roadside. I had recently moved and the paper box was not up, so the paper was put in the mailbox. The mail carrier throwed it out and the wind and rain did the rest. I paid for this newspaper and if there was a problem, they should have called the newspaper office.

You do not destroy what I bought and paid for. I can see it if there is no room in the box for the mail, but that was not the case. How did they become government property? I bought the box, the post, and put it up. It belongs to me! How did we let the so-called "government" take over our lives so completely? We have no right to control our own mailbox? That is pathetic. Its little things like this that makes you aware of just how many rights you do not have.

We need to get the government out of our lives. Show me what they have ever done for us except take our taxes and give them to every foreign country know to man and allow companies to send all our jobs out of the country. If our money was kept here, we would have no poverty. There would be plenty of money to help the less fortunate, and that includes the veterans they walk over on their way to work every day and just let them lay there. And we would have jobs galore.

Sure we might have to pay a little more for the things we buy, but it would be worth it. Any person that wants to move their business out of this country for cheap labor, I just have one thing to say to them. When you move your company, you go too, and with a one-way ticket. Sell you goods to other countries. Don't send them back here. Allowing things like this to happen is going to be the downfall of this country. We don't need to worry about terrorist. Our government is doing their job for them in royal fashion!

November 24, 2002

Planning Commission

It seems the homeowner's, churches, businesses and farms in Amherst are about to lose some of their rights as of December 4, thanks to the Planning Commission with the blessing of the Board of Supervisors. The puzzling thing here is this. Why have they been advertising for all these businesses to relocate to Amherst County and now they decide they do not want any more growth in the "town" of Amherst? The whole purpose of growth is to obtain money for the county. And now the town of Amherst is off limits? Seems like some influence peddling going on here?

As for the comments about "no one showing up for the meetings," many do not know about them. Where are the notices? Hidden in a column or are they written in cryptic? I read the paper all on the time and I see very few. And, what about the taxpayers who do not get a paper? Send out flyers with your intentions on them and I bet the people will come. You have no right to complain about the cost, you are using our money. If you keep on pushing people up against a wall, you are asking for problems.

People will take so much and then they will push back. Let the homeowners, churches, businesses and farmers alone. They have the right to do as they please with what they own. You should dwell on how to salvage some of our tax dollars on the blunder you have already made with the shell building, for one example. Maybe Jerry Falwell would be interested in it. He will need a home base here when he starts to take over this county like he is doing Lynchburg. You may control the taxpayers as of now, but when he comes, he will be calling the shots. And if you think you can control him like you are trying to control us, you had better think again.

December 27, 2002

A "New" Year?

I heard from a few taxpayers recently and was given some unbelievable information. I understand some officials are talking about putting up another shell building right beside the one they already have. How absurd can some people get? Not with my tax dollars! I will go on record right now and let them know that little fact. People stand up and be heard. They are counting on you doing nothing. I am glad so many people showed up at the meeting about the barking dogs. That is the way it should be at all of the meetings. One thing puzzles me though.

People will show up when an issue concerns their pets, but not when it concerns their tax dollars. Can anyone explain why that is? With the New Year here, we need to start looking out for each other. Stand up and speak out when things happen to other taxpayers, which doesn't seen fair. We are blessed with "freedom of speech" and many do not use it unless it concerns just them. With that way of thinking, we will never get ahead. We need to look out for each other. That is the way to really change things. Start with the next county election. We have a few good officials, but most have "wore out their welcome." We need independent people who will represent the taxpayers and not the just the wealthy, the lobbyists, and the "influence peddlers."

Also, someone in the county is not doing his or her homework. And that is costing us money. I am talking about the Centra Health project in Brockman Park. To bring in more tax revenue, they sell them the land and when they get around to the issue of taxes, they are exempt. A fatal error on someone's part. Someone should have checked to make sure they paid taxes or sell to someone who would. The lawyers for the county should have been on top of that one. What happened to legal counsel? So, look out people, we will be made to make up that loss. Let's start working on the next election. Our survival depends on it.

December 29, 2002

Lobbyist

I recently read about House Bill 1212, which would allow mobile homes and module homes in residential areas, if passed, and some county officials are against it. If it fails, the bottom line is this. If you are not rich enough to afford a site built house, then you are out of luck. This is outright discrimination. They are discriminating against people who cannot afford anything better. A residential area is just that. If a person owns the property, they should be able to put an "outhouse" on it if they want too. Any type of residence should be allowed. The county did not pay a dime on it and no one gave them the authority to tell you what to do with your own property. They just took it.

If the ordinance is for controlling growth, what a joke. They had better pray for growth to fund their pet projects. They are not getting it from me. I am getting a little sick and tired of my tax dollar being wasted. People and businesses don't even want to move here anymore. But, if they like high taxes, discrimination, wasted tax dollars, patched roads, bad drinking water and very few rights, then this is the place for them.

As for hiring lobbyist, give me a break. I don't want my money wasted that way either. We need to get them out of government, not hire more. They are no different than special interest groups. How stupid can some people get? Lobbyist will say anything they are told too, for money. They are not looking out for anyone but themselves and those who hired them. A few chosen words that "lobbying" is called in the Legal Dictionary: Influence, pressure, persuasion, pushing, instigation and pulling strings. Gee, those words sound familiar. If the board wants a voice, they should go do the lobbying themselves. It's another waste of our tax dollars that could be put too much better use. But, what do I know? Just wait till the next election.

Chapter 4

2003

January 16, 2003

911 Center

Many taxpayers are questioning the new $777,000 Emergency Services Center that is to be built. Their concern: We are in no position to spend that much of the taxpayer's money on a "new" building as of now. Is there some desperate reason it needs to be in Amherst?

Why not take the shell building we have already paid for and fix it up. Surely it shouldn't cost $777,000, but if it did, we would get a lot more for our money. It is big enough to hold the Emergency Services Center, the Monelison Rescue Squad and the Fire Department. They should all be together anyway. How long do you plan to keep them "cooped up like sardines in a can" in those little buildings they are in now? They would have plenty of room for growth in the shell building and what is just as important, free up the congestion at Amelon Elementary School. The school could then use the buildings they leave. It is way too congested there and an access road will not help the problem that much. It makes perfect sense to me.

Sooner or later the Fire Dept. and Rescue Squad will need larger quarters and it will cost us way more than $777,000. The county officials should know that after all these years no one wants the shell building. May as well put it to good use. We've made it this far without the money it would generate; actually, we're losing money just trying to keep it standing. Having someone in there would help.

And while I am on the subject of the Fire Dept. and Rescue Squads; the county gets by like "thieves in the night" since they pay them nothing. I think they should be paid a salary. Would the supervisors work for nothing? Yeah, right! And they do not even put their lives on the line. Do away with wasteful spending and put that money to a more practical use. Let the people controlling our money be volunteers and the Fire Dept. and Rescue Squads be paid. Now that really makes sense!

As to be expected, they didn't go for this.

February 9, 2003

Lobbyist Not Needed

If there was any doubt that we need a change in some of our county officials in Amherst, it flew out the window when the Board decided to retain a certain lobbyist. Now, I have nothing against anyone involved in this mess, but this has got to be about the stupidest decision the Board has ever made. Do they have any idea what this is saying about those who handle the county's business? Why would you hire anyone who worked for a person who has broken the law, especially if it is a politician? That right there is guilt by association. If you are caught with someone who has broken the law, you go to jail along with them. And the jails are full of those poor souls.

But what happens here in Amherst County? The board says, "you can break a law at the state level, but come on down and work for us." This is totally absurd. Why don't they just go ahead and hire a drug dealer, pimp of some other hardened criminal? If you are going to spend the money, you may as well "hire the best." You could not look any worse. The next thing you know, we will have law-breakers in office out in Amherst. Actually, if you did a little poking around, you might just find some already out there.

Decisions like this are not in the best interest of the citizens of Amherst County. The point I am trying to make is this, you never put anyone in public office that is not "squeaky-clean," certainly not these days. How much worse is it going to get here in the county before people decide to change things? I hope for all our sakes, it will be soon.

This is some message we are sending our children. You are supposed to be punished for wrongdoing, not rewarded. The sinkhole is getting very deep out in Amherst and the whole state is laughing as they sink lower.

March 1, 2003

Budget

I understand from reading *The Amherst New-Era Progress* that real estate taxes are falling flat. No growth. Gee, really? Why doesn't that surprise anyone in Amherst County? Do they not know that we have already figured that out? Do they really think all those restrictions they have placed on everything are helping? No way!

People are sick and tired of being told what they can and cannot do with about everything they own. Who wants to move to Amherst County and be right in the middle of a sinking ship? No one wants to move here anymore. They want to move out. And whose fault is that? Our local government and some of the insane things they want to spend money on, when there is none. Better get use to it, because taxes are going to get flatter. Maybe if they get flat enough, they will give up and leave office. You just wait until the state taxes come in. With so many people out of work, you will be lucky to get a dime back from the state.

As for the proposed budget, no salary increases now. If they do not want to work for what they are paid now, there are plenty of people out here that would gladly take their job. No help with health insurance either. The taxpayers have no one to pay our increases but us. And what makes county officials so important that they cannot pay their own too? And, as for those voting machines, if the state "mandates" that we use them, let the state or the "corrupt boys on up the latter" buy them. Leave our local money alone.

March 5, 2003

Ticket

This letter is in reference to an incident that happened on 3-3-03. A deputy, looking to make his quota, I presume, stopped my son and ticketed him for not coming to a complete stop at the to top of Amelon Road where it goes into Dixie Airport. This is totally insane? The road there is closed. There are only about 3 homes down the hill and until they open the new road, it should be considered a side street. There are exceptions to every rule. Anyone with common sense knows that's a yield spot. Every driver and myself slow down and look down the hill, but no one comes to a complete stop, unless a car is coming. My son has always owned up to his mistakes like a man, but this time, this was nothing but harassment. They stopped him because he was driving a big-wheeled Bronco and they though he was a teenager, discrimination plain and simple.

If the county needs money that bad, cut some of their jobs instead of writing bogus tickets. Some spend too much time sitting around the restaurants anyway. There are some fine deputies in the county and they do a great job. But, send these "quota seekers" after criminals, drug dealers and not target every young person around for stupid crap. This has been going on a long time and it's time it is stopped. This county is getting to be about as corrupt as some of the criminals locked up in the jail. And, don't tell me I do not know what I am talking about, because I have been watching things go on in this county for 62 years and have pretty much left well enough alone, until they target my son unfairly.

And for the record, I do not intend to come to a complete stop at Amelon and Dixie Airport Road until the new road is open, unless of course, a car is coming. I also will be weaving in and out of my lane on Izaak Walton Road and every other road I travel. I am not intoxicated and I am not high on pot. But, I have no intention of tearing up my 91 Aerostar, dark green in color, license plate Wendy 5, because the state is too cheap to fix the roads. Now if they want to pay the repair bills, I will gladly keep in my lane. And, since they are determined to write tickets, sit out on 29 and nail those who run the red lights and often times kill people. That right there would be the "motherlode." Spare the undeserving.

March 20, 2003

Just Stop at the Stop Sign

I'd like to respond to last week's letter by Wendy Nash wailing at the Sheriff's Department for ticketing her son for not stopping at a stop sign. It really is quite a simple concept:

Stop at a stop sign and you won't get a ticket.

Just think. If people didn't willfully choose to disobey traffic laws because they felt like it, there would be no quota, and the deputies would be available to go after criminals, drug dealers, and "sit out on 29 and nail those who run the red light and often times kill people." Running a stop sign, whether you deem it necessary or not is "stupid crap" on the part of the driver, not the deputy ticketing them.

Try this. Approach the stop sign while applying even pressure on the brake pedal until the vehicle comes to a complete stop. That means not moving. Look left. Look right. Proceed on to the destination, then get a grip.

Beth Franklin
Madison Heights

March 21, 2003

Stop Signs

I stated last week it was unfair to target young people. The reason I know that is the case is as follows: I have spoken with an older taxpayer that yielded at a stop sign and was only given a warning. Not ticketed. And he is far from the only one that this has happened too. Now why was that, because he was not a young person? Or is it because the deputies can ticket who they like and warn the others? Looks like age discrimination to me. If not, I would like an explanation why so many young people are ticked and older people just warned. That should be the other way around, because us older folks have been around long enough to really know better.

In two days, I have witnessed a Virginia State Dept. of Highways truck "yield" at a stop sign, two County School Buses "yield" at stop signs and many vehicles. Would someone enlighten me as to why they chose to disobey traffic laws? It's because stop signs are where yield signs belong. That's why. And you expect young people not to do the same? As for running a stop sign, there was no "running" involved in my son's case. Crawling would be a more appropriate word.

There's a big difference between running and crawling. What is the purpose of coming to a "complete stop" when there is "nothing" coming in any direction? Does the state have a logical answer to that question? There is no safety issue here. Is it a money making gimmick? Or could it be to save the life of the little bug coming up the road that nobody can see? Why do subdivision and side roads in the county have stop signs instead of yield signs? And I am not talking about major highway's here. If not to make money, then what? Why are some subdivisions without any signs at all? They can just do as they please?

And worst of all, the busiest road in the county has no sign either, and that would be at the Coolwell Road Dumpster. That road has more traffic than the Capital Beltway. Who ever makes the decisions on yield vs. stop signs on side roads needs to reconsider. And, every maintained road in the county should at least have a yield sign or take down the rest. What's good for the goose is good for the gander.

March 28, 2003

Deputies

While talking with some taxpayers, the following questions have come up.

1. Why do some of the restaurants in the county give the deputies and the sheriff half-price on the food they eat while on duty? Why do they not give the same luxury to the fire department, rescue squad and to be perfectly honest, every county employee in Amherst? How does that make them feel? Anyone ever considered that? The other county employees work just as hard and they should be given the same consideration. Of course, they cannot sit around with a gun on the hip and protect a persons business. But they can save your life, save your building from burning down, and bring in dollars.

2. Why do the deputies spend so much time at the Monelison Fire Dept. and Rescue Squad? And what's with this washing their cars there? I thought that was supposed to be done by trustees out in the jail. Some folks have brought attention to the fact that they should be patrolling the roads a lot more.

3. I also understand there are no deputies up on Slap Creek Road off of #635. Why is that? The only time they are seen in that area is when the dispatch center radios them after an incident happens. Folks up there pay the same taxes as the rest of us and deserve the same service.

4. Why aren't the Sheriff Dept. cars left at the jail when the deputies are off duty? Since the board wants more money, park those cars, with the exception of Deputy Viar, (with his dog), and save a bundle. They should not be for personal use. People that take advantage of the system after they are hired waste a lot of money in this county. And they all know who they are. But you can blame the Board of Supervisors for that. They sign off on all of this stuff.

5. Why did the Board use our money to buy Mr. Ball a new car when a used one would do? How many of the taxpayers knew that? Check and see who is up for re-election in November, check their voting record and if necessary, replace them. One by one we can get control of out tax dollars. Put the women out there. They sure could not do any worse. And, please do not shoot the messenger because you do not like the message.

April 10, 2003

Budget

First, I would like to say I am stating facts and am criticizing no one. I find it interesting how the County Administrator and the Board blames the county's budget problems on the state. What did the taxpayers get from the $25,000 they spent on the lobbyist? Nothing, and I am sure the state wasn't behind that! With the country in a recession, right now we can do without new school buses, trails, docks, new cars for officials, pay raises, new building and some employees sitting around in Amherst doing nothing. And I heard mention of a pay raise? Who gets a pay raise during a recession? Most people thank God for the jobs they still have, let alone getting a pay raise. If the county employees can't live with what they make, there are a lot of qualified people out of work who would love to have their jobs.

As for higher real estate and personal property taxes, how do you think people out of work are going to pay higher taxes on anything? The bottom line is this and it doesn't take a rocket scientist to figure this out. With the World Trade Center coming down, the stock market bottoming out, companies going under and people losing their jobs, anybody with common sense could have seen the state cuts coming, or, no money at all. But they still went ahead and spent $777,000 on a new 911 center that could have waited.

It's not how much money you have, but how you spend it. And, the officials in Amherst should think long and hard before they raise taxes or cut services to anyone or they will be the ones looking for a job. If you don't like the wasteful spending, elect three new supervisors in November that will work with the taxpayers. You would then have a majority.

April 18, 2003

Comments

It seems some readers are not reading my letters very carefully, so I will try to clear things up a bit. In the college dictionary "criticize" has more than one definition. The one I prefer: To judge the merits and faults of, analyze and evaluate. The important part here is analyze and evaluate. Now if in doing that, someone is offended, that is just too bad. In my letter on the stop signs, I asked questions, analyzed and evaluated. I "applauded", not "criticized" the one VDOT truck and the two school buses for using their heads and thinking for themselves when there was a clear road and no danger in "yielding" at the stop signs. Under some circumstances that is ok. No one would ever get a driver's license unless they knew the meaning of a stop sign. That doesn't mean they are going to stop when it is safe to yield.

As for the questions pertaining to the deputies, let me first say this. I have known Sheriff Ayers since he was a boy and he has the nicest parents anyone could ever ask for. I applaud the Sheriff's Department for the work they do. I know what goes on there, as I went to the first Citizen's Police Academy. And, my beef is not with the Sheriffs Department, but one deputy who made a wrong call.

They are only human and some make mistakes just like the rest of us. But, I still have the right to ask questions on behalf of other people that would rather not sign their names for fear of losing their job. So I offered to be the messenger.

What does that say about the county when people can't ask questions without fear of retribution? As for "doing research," those to whom the questions pertain should do the research and provide the answers to the readers. A public forum is where all can get those answers if they choose to respond. And, to those who do not like my letters, no one is forcing you to read them. If you do not like what you are reading, just skip that part or put the newspaper down. I still plan to ask questions, analyze and evaluate things and many others as I see them. If you choose to criticize me or "poke fun" at me for doing that, you go right ahead, I can handle it, but I do not plan on stopping.

May 9, 2003

Firearms?

Well, another example of our incompetent legal system. Being as my son wanted to enlist in the military, he was checked through the FBI. And guess what? According to them, information obtained through the always-correct justice system in Amherst, is this. They have my son convicted for "discharging a firearm in a dwelling." The truth is this: in his younger years he was fined for throwing EGGS from a roadway. That's right eggs. Or, to be perfectly correct, a "missile." But, how can anyone confuse eggs and firearms? There is no argument as to whether he was guilty of throwing eggs. The problem is the county did not inform the FBI that this was the case and not "discharging a firearm in a dwelling."

Common sense tells you, throwing eggs is not the same as "discharging a firearm in a dwelling" and surely shouldn't be given to the FBI as such. If he was convicted for "throwing eggs," it should be listed as that. **Convicted of throwing eggs.** No matter what statue it falls under. The FBI had the wrong information and it came from Amherst. Imagine what the military thought when that bit of info showed up on their computer screen. A word of warning to anyone convicted of anything in Amherst. You had better make sure the information the FBI has on you is correct. You can rest assured Amherst can't get it straight. If it hadn't been for the military, this "little bitty" mistake would probably never have been found. What a go, Amherst!

This one error could ruin a person's life. Who ever was responsible better clear it up. And I want it in writing. And, this goes way past the Board of Supervisors, straight up to the courts. If someone typing the info into the computer did this, they should be out of a job. This was nothing short of providing false information to the FBI and I do not want to hear "it was an honest mistake." When pigs fly! Who else is running for re-election this November???? It seems the whole house needs cleaning!

May 16, 2003

Trips!

As far as the trips our "officials" took to the Greenbriar, I have a few questions. First off, I did not pay taxes to have it spent on vacations. Now they can say what they want about the so-called "benefits." How do these people live with themselves? Do they not have a conscience? How do they show their faces after this? Where do these people get off? Who cares if the whole state does it? If you can't use your own money, do not go. I am sure the information was written on a computer somewhere; track it down and send everyone copies. I know reading is not as much fun, but it is a whole lot cheaper!

Tax dollars were not paid by us to be wasted. The only thing any current local government official has done lately is raise taxes, pass every kind of zoning law they could come up with, take away our rights to make decisions for ourselves and waste our money. And they call this a "free" country?

Another thing of importance is this: Pave Izaak Walton Road, from one end to the other. It is patched the entire length. New pavement has been put on Amelon, Dixie Airport and Coolwell. We pay the same taxes and we want the same roads. You have a foot on both sides in gravel that we can't use. Pave that too. As it is now, it's no wider than a "pig path." Most of the problem comes from those garbage trucks from Satan's home. They drive like bats out of Satan's home and hog the road. Always running the yellow line because they are too wide. It is a miracle no one has been killed by one of them yet. Ever consider those school buses?

Until the road is improved, find another way to the dump for those "monstrosities" called garbage trucks. There are others ways; it just takes a little longer. This is a very dangerous road with them on it, so get those wide speed demons under control, give us a decent road and stop wasting out money. It's going to be scarce next tax time!

June 12, 2003

Criticism Unwarranted

In response to the criticism of Wendy Nash by Lynette Staples of Lynchburg (May 29, 2003 issue), I WISH Amherst County had more Wendy's who would speak up about what goes on in this county. I would be the first in line to vote for Wendy should she run for any office in this county. We certainly need some new blood and someone representing the people and voting as the people they represent wish instead of what the county CEO's want. Our present Board of Supervisors by no means represents the people who elected them.

Since Ms. Staples lives in Lynchburg, she cannot possibly have the foggiest idea of how bad and unfair some things are in the county. She probably thinks Wendy exaggerates on some of the things she writes about, but I can assure you that she does not. By the way, I do not even know Wendy, but I do admire her guts to stand up for what she sees wrong and call attention to it. The way our Board of Supervisors and our law enforcement run this county, I almost think I live in the town in the movie, "Walking Tall".

Shortly after reading Wendy's letter about her son being charged with running a stop sign on Dixie Airport Rd., I came upon this very sign myself. Since the road is CLOSED due to work on the new bypass, it is perfectly ridiculous to have a STOP sign there in the first place. And, Ms. Staples, how would you like to have an incorrect charge on your permanent files? I know of a similar incident in which the wronged party was not even aware of the incorrect charge until the then presiding Commonwealth Attorney said the "statue of limitations had expired", so the party was not allowed to appeal something they were unaware of. I have lived in other cities and states prior to moving to Amherst Count, so I can tell you that a lot of things are not right in this county, just as Wendy points out.

I am glad that Wendy takes the time and effort to bring these things to our public's attention. I wish more people would do the same.

KEEP UP THE COOD WORK, WENDY!

Joyce Pendleton
Madison Heights

I was unable to obtain the letter sent to the newspaper by Ms. Staples.

June 18, 2003

Stop Signs on Dogwood Drive

Why put a "stop" sign where a "yield" sign would do? For example: If VDOT can explain why a stop sign instead of a yield sign is needed at the end of a road, where you can see up both hills for approximately ¼ of a mile on each side, I will be glad to stop asking this question. Anyone who would like to view this particular spot, take Dixie Airport Road, off 29 North, to Possum Island Road and hang a left. (There is no stop sign to turn left, but there sure is a stop sign coming back out if you turn right. Make any sense?) Travel a few hundred feet and hang a right onto Dogwood Drive. Go to the bottom of the hill, stop and look left and right. Try to figure out why a stop sign is there. This is a yield spot. If you crawl through a stop sign, they can fine you and ruin your driving record to boot. If you crawl through a yield sign there is no fine.

And further more, it's a slap in the face of intelligent people. I do not like to be presumed dumb. If some idiot wants to pull out in front of a car, a stop sign is not going to stop them. This is just another attempt to bleed the taxpayer dry of every dollar they have. If I am not mistaken, VDOT works for the taxpayers and as such we have the right to have any question we ask, "answered."

But, a month ago I emailed the Lynchburg VDOT who handles this area and in Amherst, and even the VDOT office in Richmond and asked, "how do you decide where to put a stop vs. a yield sign" and no one will even reply. They probably cannot come up with an answer. They just stick stop signs where they want to and lay in wait for their prey? I will find out, if it takes retaining an attorney and have the bill send to VDOT. It is a shame taxpayer dollars have to be spent to find out the answer to a question that VDOT could provide free by communicating with those who employ them. Some may not care about little questions like this, but in the big picture they are very important.

June 19, 2003

Unhappy With The Local Officials

On June 12, 2003, Joyce Pendleton wrote in the letter to the editor, the way the Board of Supervisors and law enforcement ran the county, she almost thought she lived in the town in the movie "Walking Tall."

As for our law enforcement, I myself feel more like we are still living in the early 60s when punks went out and took innocent people and killed them and half the town would cover up for them.

Living in Amherst County is no different. It is sad to live in a county where a human was burned to death and know your sheriff's department and Commonwealth's Attorney did so little to see he got any real justice for his cruel death.

Joyce Pendleton said it right when she said it was time for soon new blood to take office in Amherst. I agree with her 100 percent. Take out the old and put in some new. Then maybe when you are victims you will be treated like one and not treated as if you were the murderer.

I feel it is time for them to stop hiding behind their closed doors and do right by everyone, not just some, for murder was murder.

So, Wendy Nash, if you ever run for office I will be there to vote for you. Keep on writing your letters and Joyce Pendleton, I could have said it no better. I enjoyed your letter.

Shirley Stinnett
Monroe

July 9, 2003

Big Business

The Board of Supervisors is supposed to look out for the lower income taxpayers as well as the upper class. But that is not happening in Amherst County. The majority of people who support the Board are the ones who have enough money to pay higher taxes. Keep the county simple and you will not need so many tax dollars. You should be getting rich off of Wal-Mart and that is the only "big business" we need. What we do not need are people who are gradually buying up every inch of land they can get their hands on here in the county and trying to turn it into "big business." Expand the ones we already have. Not build more.

We should keep up what we have here in the county. Check out our beautifully landscaped highway. If they had taken our money they helped themselves to for their little getaway, and put it toward beautifying Rt. 29, we would at least had something to smile about on our way home from work.

We should not be asked to sacrifice our simple life for "big business." If the Supervisors want "big business," they should move to Richmond and build all you want. But give us simple folks the right to live our simple lives. Stop the buying and taking of our land and creating "big business" where it is not wanted. We have rights too, but we'll have to fight for them, because they are not going to just hand them over.

Seeking Office

According to an article in the *Lynchburg News and Advance*, some on the Board of Supervisors have a misconception that needs to be cleared up about why no one is seeking to serve on the board.

We have "simple folks" that know how to take care of money and work long hours, but do not have the money and influence to get elected. That's why they do not seek the office. Not because they think the board is doing a good job. Trust me. The board is way off base there.

We do need some on the board with a college education. But, just as important, we need some "common sense" candidates to represent the "simple living" folks. A well-educated upper class person is just not on the same level as us when it comes to what we simple people want and need. And, we do not need them telling us what is best for us.

To really make this county work, we need our "little" farmers, next-door neighbor etc. to balance out the board. People should not be elected just because they are "bought and paid for" by someone, and belong to a certain party. The way you get elected here in Amherst County is by having money and influence. The majority of taxpayers have neither. So you tell me how the simple folks can be fairly represented when they haven't the "means" to get elected?

August 15, 2003

Rights

With what is going on in many countries, freedom means more today than ever. We should have the right to live as we wish in this so-called "free country." We are freer than most, but we are not truly free.

We are like trained animals, obeying the governments ever rule. All of these zoning ordinances they are sneaking in here and there, well, we have more than enough. They should not have the right to force people to comply with their every whim. If people choose too, fine.

They are no different from "special interest" groups. They have ruined this country. Many in Congress are "paid off" to get all of these little whims hid in the laws they pass. They are looking out for no one but themselves and their deep pockets. We did not put them in office for that reason.

You can try to make things better in the world today, but you should not have the right to force people who want to live as they wish to buckle down to every stupid law. This is the government from the local all the way up to the federal, sneaky as they come. And they have the nerve to talk about other countries.

We the people need to get rid of most of those currently in office and elect new representatives that are accountable to the people. Demand they get rid of "free trade" and create jobs in this country. Demand they stop interfering in our everyday life by passing every little law they want us to follow. They should be watched like hawks. The first misstep, have them removed. God gave the government the ability to improve things. God did not give the government the right to force us to accept those improvements.

August 26, 2003

Weeds

The latest disaster to hit Amherst County is weeds and tall grass. Since they are low on money, the zoning board is going after people who let them grow over 12 inches. And this includes grass too. Now, what are the weeds hurting? You take all of them away and all of the snakes and undesirables will be on our front porches. Weeds serve an ecological purpose. If people do not like the weeds, don't look at them. They were here before us.

Article IV Sec 13-57 (b) Commercial/ Industrial or Institutional Property says: It shall be unlawful for any owner of a vacant developed property to permit growth of any grass or weed of more than 12 inches in height. Who gave the state the right to implement this stuff? What does the zoning board have to do with other peoples businesses? The county is getting plenty of money from the taxes they pay.

I find it interesting that the zoning board didn't propose this until after they contracted someone to cut the land around the Amelon Shell Building. That place has looked like a jungle for years. They made sure their butts were covered before they attempted this. My land, my weeds! That's the way I look at it. Next, It will be our yards. If we have to live by these stupid ordinances, so should every county building, vacant or not. And who fines them?

The people did not vote to accept all of these stupid ordinances in the Code of Virginia. A few elected to speak for everyone and just made them up. Where are our rights? The Constitution did not give the state or the county the right to pass this junk. And it sure wasn't on any ballot. We do not even own our own land. If you do not pay your real estate taxes, they just take it and leave you with nothing. When will it ever end? Not until the taxpayers stand up and take back our rights.

Parts of this letter were deleted. Did not keep a copy of the printed letter, unfortunately.

August 30, 2003

Gays

With all the attention about the gay issue, I put this to you to think about. First, I am not for gays and I am not against gays. I stand squarely in the middle. I pass no judgment on anyone because of his or her lifestyle. Gays are supposed to have rights too and some are very gifted and caring people.

The Bible does say that God is against the gay lifestyle and no one should disobey God. But, I have news for you; it is done every day. Ever hear of the Ten Commandments? Thou shall not kill, commit adultery, covert their neighbors wife or steal, to name a few. These are also sins that are broken everyday and there is no uprising over them.

It is up to God to punish those who disobey him. The gays will never destroy our country; the government is doing quite a good job of that. You can pass all the laws you want, but the bottom line is this: No law will ever change what they believe or practice. Live and let live and leave the gays to answer to God. They have been here since time began and they will be when it ends. People should be worried more about where their next meal is coming from and not people's lifestyles. Get on with your own lives. They are shorter than you think.

September 7, 2003

Left Out Sentences

The following sentences were edited out of my (Aug, 26) letter. Since it was over 250 words (which most letters were) someone decided to take some of the sentences out. But, they took out the most important ones. Which are:

1. Since they are low on money, the zoning board is going after people who let weeds and tall grass grow over 12." (Everyone knows it about money. Do away with the fines and see how many ordinances they pass).

2. What does the zoning board have to do with other people's businesses?

3. The county is getting plenty of money from the taxes we pay.

4. They made sure their butts were covered before attempting this. (In reference to the passing of the weed control ordinance, which included the Amelon Industrial Park.

5. We do not even own our own land. If you do not pay your taxes, they just take your land and leave you with nothing. Is this not the truth?

Has someone from across the street pressured the newspaper? Or could it be because *The News and Advance* bought the paper out? Why leave out the negative things? If they can't stand the heat get out of the kitchen. I plan to start my own web page and post my letters there also. Then not only will Amherst see them, but the whole wide world. That should turn the heads of anyone thinking about coming here. People beware! Research those ordinances first and know there are more to come, with fewer rights.

The *Amherst New-Era Progress* would not publish this letter for whatever reason.

October 5, 2003

Weed Ordinance

I have been wondering if the ordinance pertaining to the height of grass has gone into effect? If so, the shell building is in violating of this ordinance. Now the question, if the county fines others for violations, who fines the county? Does the county fine itself or are they exempt from the ordinance? They still own the building. What's good for the goose is good for the gander! The taxpayers have a right to know the answer to this question. And, Mr. Carter, good luck on getting any ordinance appealed. You may have to go to The United States Supreme Court for that.

November 1, 2003

Vicious Dogs Running Loose

Since the elections are over, its back to bringing attention to things that needs changing in Amherst County. This problem with the dogs has been going on for years and it's all over the county. I am glad some of the taxpayers are finally standing up and saying, "Enough is enough." If we would speak out on all of the issues, this county would finally be heading in the right direction.

I find it appalling the court date for Mrs. Cash has been moved back to December. According to Mr. David, they want to "obtain information on the history of the property." This has to be some kind of joke. The only information they need to know, they already have people in the neighborhood are in danger now. They may be dead by December. Then the county will be sued, that's for sure.

All the information that the courts need to know is that people are in harm's way. History has nothing to do with what needs to be done about the dog problem. Do they think the dogs care about any history? The people involved here should be the one's to inform the courts. You don't need lawyers that the taxpayers will have to pay for. It sure would be a lot cheaper. If anything happens to one of our citizen's because of the dogs, Amherst will be on the front page of every newspaper in the state. Who will want to move into a county where this goes on?

November 3, 2003

Walmart

In response to the editorial about Wal-Mart in the 10-31 issue of *The Lynchburg News and Advance*, I have these facts to convey.

First, people are innocent until proven guilty. At least that's the way it should be. If they did do wrong, I am sure they will take their medicine like good little boys and girls.

Second, the reason they can keep their prices so low is that they buy vast amounts of merchandise and can afford to sell it cheaper.

Third, I took you up on finding something made in the U.S.A. in Wal-Mart. That was not hard to do. Check out these departments. Candy, grocery, house wares, shoes, paper goods, bakery, lawn and garden, jewelry, pets, men's, women's, children's, fabric and crafts, domestics, tire and lube, health and beauty, hardware, automotive, sporting goods and toys. Gee, that's the whole darn store.

Fourth, people are not outraged because with the country practically in a depression, they will shop for the best price. If that is Wal-Mart so be it.

Fifth, as far as loss of jobs goes, put the blame squarely where it belongs. That is the "good ole" politician's that passed the trade agreement and send our hard earned money to every country in the world. Our government will be the downfall of this country, not Wal-Mart.

And, sixth, the mom and pop stores are just fine. I grew up in them. But, they had the same opportunity to prosper as Sam Walton. He had a vision and you know the rest. ("Sam Walton, *The Model Manager of Wal-Mart*" by Kelly Fitzgerald on the Internet.) He was not born with a silver spoon in his mouth. Wal-Mart has given money to many charities and helped many in the process.

As for shoddy tactics, look in the mirror. If the paper can be sued for publishing what they cannot prove as true, this is certainly one of those times.

Chapter 5

2004

January 3, 2004

Car Dealers Tax

I cannot find any logic whatsoever in the latest decision by the Board of Supervisors concerning the merchant's capital tax. Instead of charging the dealers on what they sell, they get greedy and try to make them pay it on their inventory. I heard this mentioned the first part of last year, so when they say they did not have time to vote on it, that's poppycock.

So, what happened? Instead of taxing the dealers on what they sell, and receiving some tax money, they wind up with nothing. This is money that could have been used for the budget that now will have to come out of the taxpayer's pockets.

There is one of two things you can do here. Let the car dealers pay on what they sell OR tax every merchant, whether it be a cattle farmer, grocery store restaurant, retail store etc. on their inventory.

The dictionary says a merchant is as follows. "A person who deals in the purchase and sale of goods (a licensed merchant), dealer, seller, buyer, trader, retailer, trafficker, tradesman, jobber, wholesaler, shopkeeper, industrialist, capitalist, chandler, vendor, huckster, middleman, salesman, saleswoman, hawker, financier, purchaser and peddler". So where do they get off targeting just the car dealers? If you really want to see some action, try pulling this on the antique dealers and Wal-Mart. Until there is a "big change" in the local county officials, things are going to get a lot worse. Can't wait to see what's coming next!

March 4, 2004

Outhouse

The town of Amherst has made a big mistake in removing the "outhouse" the Cancer Society was using to raise money. If I read correctly, it was on the towns "right-of-way." Why didn't they just move it back into to what is "suppose" to be the homeowners yard?

This was a prop for God's sake. We are living in Amherst County here, not Hollywood. No one is forcing people to look into other people's yards. We should all build "outhouses" and place them on our land in support of the Cancer Society. And they will stay there, unless, the county wants to be on the national news and drive even more future "growth" away. Everyone should be totally discussed with this action, ordinance or not.

The Cancer Society needs all the support it can get. Cancer is a life threatening disease and it is unbelievable that anyone would hinder their fundraising. This is a slap in the face to every cancer patient and survivor. As a cancer survivor myself, I find this action by the county official's completely appalling.

Of all the things to support, the whole county should take this under their wing and promote the fund-raiser as a matter of life and death, in which it may very well be for some. What will it take to wake some people up as to what is really important in life? Maybe a bout with cancer will do it! What a go Amherst!

May 23, 2004

Dumpster Road

I would like to know why the county doesn't buy this land that the real estate developers want to see declared abandoned? They could turn it into future subdivisions and make a bundle selling the lots. You know, every year land just increases in value. Realty companies develop them for the money, so why shouldn't the county? It could be a small fortune. You don't need to put it up for auction and sell it to developers for nothing. When is "enough money is enough" for some people?

The taxpayers would be glad to have a little nest egg in the form of real estate. And, if the county says they haven't the time; for the amount of money they could get from the sale of the land to benefit the taxpayers, they should find time or hire someone who can.

Also, the county has a big problem with the dumpsters on Kentmoor Farm Road. The road beside the dumpsters is completely unacceptable. It has holes that could swallow up a garbage truck. We, the taxpayers, if I am not mistaken, own the land the dump is on, the dumpsters outside and all the machinery there. Why can't they take one of our bulldozers and fix the road the way it should be and keep it that way? Can they not afford the gas prices? The taxpayers deserve better!

July 6, 2004

Bad Roads

This is in regard to the garbage truck accident on Izaak Walton Road last week. I touched on this subject in a letter in May of last year. "get those speed demons under control", "they drive like bats out of ......(hell)," "they hog the road," "they run the yellow line because they are too wide" and "it is a miracle no one has been killed."

Well, guess what? Someone almost was; if that truck had been just a little bit closer to the people he hit. What if that happened to have been a bus loaded with school children?

What will it take to wake up those responsible for the width and speed of this road? Widen it or move large trucks off of it. Lower the speed limit. 45 is to fast for a road this narrow. Dixie Airport is twice as wide and their speed limit is only 35. Make any sense? Just as many homes and kids on Izaak Walton.

Are they just going to sit back and do nothing as usual? Until lawsuits hit them and we all pay through the nose? People need to speak up on this issue before some of their loved ones are killed.

Also, how much money did the taxpayers lose on the sale of the shell building? No price was mentioned or what it is going to cost us in the deals they made to get them to move here. Publish that information! Everyone one would like to know the answer.

July 22, 2004

The Shell Building

In the July 15 issue of the *Amherst New-Era Progress*, the Board of Supervisors had a "notice of intent to dispose of property and all the improvements." This was of course the shell building on Amelon Road. A hearing was to be held for the public's input on July 20. But, in the July 8 issue, it stated the property had been sold July 1. That was 20 days before the hearing was scheduled. What was the hurry? Now, how can the taxpayers of this county have a say as to their thoughts on the sale, when it was sold right out from under them? We are talking about a million + investment here.

I think the proper word to use here is "give away." We had a building we the taxpayers paid a million dollars for (with some upkeep) that was "disposed of" for a mere $400,000. Now that was a $600,00 lost to us right there. And I suppose they gave away the 15 acres of land that went with it? Nothing of this value owned by the taxpayers should be sold without a public meeting. Something is really wrong here. How can you justify giving away way over $600,00 of the taxpayer's money? We need a serious shake-up of the decision makers in Amherst.

How much is it costing the taxpayers to develop the 100 acres they are working on now? I haven't seen a public notice on that. I do not want my tax dollars squandered without a say.

And if that wasn't bad enough, consider this. The new by-pass that will be ready in about 100 years was suppose the relieve congestion on Rt. 29. That is a joke. Sticking up all these new businesses will only add to the congestion. How do they think all the tractor-trailers going to Lowe's, Eckerd Drug, the Industrial Park, etc. will get there? And, if you want to get away from the congestion, that is not possible. Go to the mountains and then they will declare "eminent domain" and take that. You cannot win. You are being backed into a corner here.

People backed into corners do desperate things. Remember the man who wiped out most of his town with a homemade tank over zoning? There needs to be a meeting of the minds between the Board of Supervisors and those they represent. Not force all of their wishes on us. They should never be allowed to sell anything belonging to the taxpayers without the majority of us agreeing.

October 25, 2004

Sheriff's Department Pay

I ran across a letter from April of 2004 I somehow forgot to summit or it became sidetracked because of a more important one. With the next election, some things to ponder.

I have a few suggestions about a recent article about our state government, regarding the local Sheriff's Department need for an increase in pay. They say there is no money. And, that is so typical of our honest, trustworthy taxpayers bank!

The majority of our legislators do not really give a "hoot" about the taxpayer or anyone else they have to hand out money to. The only thing they care about is lining their own pockets with the money they receive from "special interest" groups, rich people who can buy their vote and supporting their "pet peeves." They care nothing about the "ordinary" taxpayer or their wishes.

The only reason they do anything for anybody is so they will be re-elected. This has been going on years and years and years and seems like it will go on forever.

The taxpayers should demand they get nothing but a salary. No special interest money, no gifts. This alone would get most of them out of office. Put this on the ballot and lets see what the taxpayers decide.

There are honest people who would run for office if they thought they could win and be a part of a majority who listens to the taxpayers; and votes for them instead of their own pocketbook's. Investigate anyone who wants to be a politician from the day they were born. Test them and see if they can be bought. Surely they won't care unless they have a few skeletons in their closet. If they protest, look out.

October 28, 2004

Birds

I am very upset over the killing of birds that have mistakenly flown into a business. I am very well aware there are safety issues involved when this happens. Especially when food is involved. I have no problem with capturing the birds and releasing them, but killing them is another matter altogether.

An employee who oversees the chemicals in a business and also moonlights as a food inspector, stated how to get rid of a "couple" of birds flying around the store. He said to take a glue board used to catch mice, dump some feed on it and they would fly down, light on it and you would have them. Now, once this happens they do not get the bird off. They are thrown in a dumpster and left to die, or killed. I find this totally unacceptable. He also wrote up the "bakery" because the birds were in the store. The birds were not in the bakery. When asked why, he said he had to "write up somebody." Now, who do these people think they are? Do they have the power to blame anyone they want to? The government must think so.

As for the health issue, what do you do when this happens in your home garden? What do the workers out in the fields do when harvesting food with no bathroom in site? Have people not heard of water? The health inspectors need to come up with a more humane way to deal with the little birds.

Stores that support the Humane Society and other organizations that are important and cares very much for any creature. This business is not ridding the world of germs by killing a "couple" of little birds. Give me a break. Businesses should find a more humane company to deal with if this is the best these people can do. Any business that promotes the killing of birds, I would have no dealings with.

I am an animal rights supporter and it is upsetting to see any bird or animal harmed. There has to be a better way. This is inhumane.

November 17, 2004

Taxes

The Board of Supervisor's desire to let businesses have a free ride on taxes at the taxpayers expense is wrong. Why did they build the new Amelon Commerce Center??? Was that not to attract businesses so the county would receive more revenue from the taxes they pay? What is wrong with this picture?

We would be far better off to run all of the businesses out of the county and go back to the '50s way of life. Then we wouldn't need a Board because there wouldn't be anything to supervise, just a quite little community where we could live in peace.

As it is now, we have to worry about where we are all going to live once our homes and land are gone. Will they put us on a reservation like the poor Indians?

The bottom line is this. Our officials have lured businesses into the county by giving them big tax breaks and now the Board of Supervisors cannot balance the budget. So they are going to try and make us pay. I think not. I for one am fed up.

When the supervisor in your district is up for re-election, think about what they are doing to us and elect someone who hasn't been in politics since the county was founded. Politics is the problem. When you change supervisors, you can then change the zoning board. Action speaks louder than words. In most cases, common sense is much more important than all the education in the world.

November 28, 2004

Businesses

Why give businesses tax breaks to relocate here? The taxpayers do not get a tax break to move to Amherst County or even the ones who have lived here all our lives and supported this county. This is unfair to the taxpayers. If the businesses cannot pay their fair share, then stay out. We the taxpayers should have the right to decide if and when to give tax breaks, because we are the ones who have built this county from scratch. This is our county. It does not belong to the Board of Supervisors.

This is where common sense comes into play. It doesn't take a rocket scientist to figure out you cannot give big tax breaks to businesses and still have enough money to run the county. Businesses should pay at least their part and not a penny less. This is a case where the "rich get richer" and the "poor get poorer" and I will let you figure out who has been coming out on the losing end, so far.

The taxpayers cannot be expected to make up what the county lost. Most of us do not have enough money to make it as it is. Poor budget management with, I might add, pork! I expect to receive the same tax break as businesses, next year. If not, that is discrimination. Giving to the rich, by taking from the poor.

December 9, 2004

Road

This letter is in regard to the Board of Supervisors meeting Tuesday, when the issue was taken up concerning the Dixie Airport Road and 130 Connector intersections. There have been many bad accidents and one death there since it opened in April.

We have a major problem here. VDOT does not want to put a stop light there until the "data" is in. Give me a big break! How absurd is that? How much more data do you need? I think over 12 accidents and one death is enough "data." How many more people will have to die there before something is done? Put the blasted stop light up now. They have to remember, they are using our money, and plenty of it. So if we say we want a stop light now, put it up now.

VDOT created this "death trap" because their engineers designed the road. This is another example of where "common sense" should have been used. They should be held accountable for accidents and deaths at this sight. If they construct an unsafe road and allow people to use it, they should be held accountable. This is negligence on the part of the state. Plain and simple.

I have one "demand" that would help out until they come to their senses. Have VDOT take some of those millions of dollars they received as a tax refund and hire some "off duty" deputies. Place one on each side of Dixie Airport Road, in shifts, twenty-four hours a day, until they put up the stoplight. And pay them "triple-time" for doing it. Then see how fast the "data" comes in. It is not up to the county to pay them, it's up to VDOT.

More people are going to die. And VDOT is responsible because they created this mess.

Chapter 6

2005

January 18, 2005

Complaints over Attire

According to the news, a Congressman is trying to get a law passed to fine people who walk around with theirs boxer shorts showing. Shorts are no big deal, but your butt showing would be. I suggest the Congressman should start at the top of this mountain. There are far more important things ahead of boxer shorts. They should change laws to rid Congress of "pork barrel spending" for starters. When Congress has accomplished this, then take on things like the g-string bathing suits that show everything. Boxers are pale in comparison.

Where does this man get off carrying on about a persons boxer shorts? Has he watched TV or been to the beach in the last decade? He has his priorities confused. And, why start this now? When a person's rights are slipping away year by year, this is insignificant. Congress needs to clean up its act first. They are now telling us we cannot say Merry Christmas any more. You want to bet? I will say it any place I chose. Those Congressmen need to go, not Merry Christmas.

Another thing I am tired of hearing about is people squabbling over wages. When you are hired you are told what you can expect in the way of wages. You know this before you take the job. No one holds a gun to your head and forces you to accept it. If you do not like the pay, walk out the door and don't let it hit you in the butt. Try to find a job elsewhere. People should be thankful they have any job, because there are many just waiting to take your place. Businesses should not have to put up with this.

Times are tough now and if people have a problem, take it to those responsible, the good ole U.S. Government. If you do not like the way things are, change Congress. That is where 99% of our problems start. If you do not vote and try to make things better, you get what you deserve. Complaining will accomplish nothing, but voting just might.

March 6, 2005

Travelers

Finally, Amherst County has it's own "first class" restaurant. I have traveled all the way to Lynchburg to find a restaurant like this and every time through a "demolition derby" of traffic. The traffic has become so bad in Lynchburg, I quit going. I love great food, but I like living better. And now we have our own great little restaurant right here in Amherst. "

The Travelers" on Main Street is absolutely fabulous. A wonderful cozy atmosphere, satellite radio that plays the best music around, and food to die for. It is a quiet, quaint little place the county has needed for a long time. The food is exceptional, the wait staff is great and as for the chef, they do not come any better. She is above "excellent." If you want a superb dining experience, give it a try.

A great big "thank you" to the owners for locating in Amherst and for bringing a chef on board that I would have to put up there with "Emil." You have achieved a "miracle" for this quiet little town and I will be dining with you from now on. And, you can take that to the bank.

March 14, 2005

Amherst News

The citizens of the U.S. are suppose to have freedom of speech, but a lot of newspapers censor you even after the First Amendment states you have that right. The problem is when you are censored; you cannot get all the information out to the citizens who may be affected, just the "sugar-coated" part. If you know an elected official is not doing their job of putting the citizens first, people should be able to bring attention to it through the media.

Last year I sent in a letter that had my web site address in it. And because I said something negative about the Board of Supervisors, you cut it out. What was the harm in the readers going to my web site? That's censorship. I know you have the option to edit letters, but that doesn't make it right? There isn't anything in my letters that could get the paper sued. And, if a letter won't fit, print it the next week, don't cut half of it out.

For some reason you will not put anything negative about the board in your newspaper, if it comes from me. You print letters from Mr. Marks and Mr. Wyland (12-16-04) about the board that are not flattering. Mine are pale in comparison. The Rucker boy's mother has written countless letters running the Sheriffs Dept. down for not finding the "right person" who burned up her son. They were printed. You edit my letters even if they say nice things. The letter I wrote about the "Travelers" was edited, so I took a copy of the letter, the way I wrote it, to them. So, how do you think that make the wait staff feel? You need to reconsider editing out parts of any letter, unless they contain threats, vulgarity, etc. If someone gets their toes stepped on that deserves it, to bad. Next time they may do better.

You are doing a disservice to your readers not giving them the entire letter. They need all of the information to make a decision about what the writer is saying. Nothing is said that could cause the paper any problems, so the local official(s), continue to pull the strings. They control everyone in Amherst, always have and will continue too, until the citizens find out just how bad it is. As long as a letter writer's "negative opinion" or questions are cut out, they never will. That is what the county officials are banking on. If you cannot bring attention to a public official's actions through the media, how do you get the word to the people?

I do not write letters for the fun of it. They always have something important to say. The letters are the only way to reach the citizens, negative or positive. That is why you do not get many "Letters to the Editor." People know they will not be printed as they were written. They tell me "why bother". Think about it.

This letter was not published either.

Art Gallery

First it was the Ten Commandments and now it is artwork. The government has come down on us again. It seems that our courthouse lobby is now off limits to artists. We cannot hang artwork in any government building because we are putting holes in the walls. Give me a break! We the taxpayers paid for everything in those buildings. They belong to us and if we want to hang artwork in them, we should have that right.

We have very talented young artist in pre-school, grade school, high school and college. Not to mention the "grass roots" artist still living in and around the county. Those public buildings were where we could display our work for the county to enjoy. Not anymore.

Some even suggested ways to hang the art without putting holes in the wall, but they still said no. But, there are pictures in them. Seen any buildings without pictures lately? There goes our "freedom of expression." What will be next? The county should be ashamed of itself. Anyone thinking of moving here beware, because they are discriminating against local artist.

To make things right, the county should donate a small building or let the artist use one that is setting around empty. Isn't there some on Main Street in Amherst? I see empty buildings all over the place. We need a little art gallery here in the county, because it would benefit people of all ages. And, it could be a nice tax right off and everyone loves those.

If anyone knows of a building, please let me or any artist know, but just as important, let the county officials know how you feel, because it is a shame that our citizens can't enjoy the work of our local artist, young and old.

"Human subtlety will never devise an invention more beautiful, more simple or more direct than does nature, because in her inventions, nothing is lacking and nothing is superfluous."
–DaVinci.

March 21, 2005

Deer Crossing

I would like to thank Paula Jones at VDOT in Lynchburg and the gentleman in Amherst, who's name I forgot, for their help in placing the "Deer Crossing" signs on Izaak Walton Road, between Partridge Creek Road and the new bridge. I urge everyone using the road to please slow down and watch for the deer, especially at night. Quite a few have been struck and killed in this section. It is not their fault that they have to wander around in everybody's yards to find something to eat. We humans have taken away their natural habitats, by building subdivisions, shopping centers, bypasses and the like.

They are not in our yards because they like us. They are there because they are hungry. And if we think they are destructive, we had better go take a good, long look in the mirror.

They are one of Gods creatures, just like us "humans". They should be respected as such. We are supposed to co-exist with wildlife, not wipe it out. Please slow down and watch out for the deer.

April 21, 2005

Jail and Humane Society

Thanks to the *Amherst New-Era Progress* for publishing the "Crime Log". There is nothing you report that could be more important than this column. You can be sure neighborhoods will be more watchful and hopefully the crime rate will go down.

Also, a few comments on two issues, the Regional Jail and Humane Society.

As for the squabble over the new jail, blame it all on the "state." They are the ones sending prisoners to "our jail." That is why there is no room. It's filled up with out-of-towners. Let them keep them in their own locality. If they do not have a jail, build one. But, don't send them here.

As for the new "Humane Society", the $2.2 million dollars of our hard earned tax dollars should be spent more wisely. A larger building is all well and good, "if," you were going to take care of the animals. But that is not what is happening. 75% are killed. It is nothing but a "concentration camp" for animals. Do you think they care about the comfort of a "state of the art" facility? No way! So if the animals don't care, whom does that leave? Spend a little less money and find homes for them. Get on the Internet. Many states have "rescue centers" to save those condemned.

I do not want my tax dollars spent on an "Auschwitz" for animals or a jail to house every criminal in the state.

May 5, 2005

More Censorship

I would like to know why there is so much censorship in Amherst County? One obvious case is when it was mentioned how much money the courts took in, in fines and court cost, they mysteriously disappeared from the Court Docket column of the newspaper. Why are the courts keeping the public from finding out how much money they make?

Also, when people are caught committing a crime, it's splashed all over the paper. Now, that is great. But when those charged go to trial, in a lot of cases, you never here the outcome. Why is that?

And, the worst problem, the Sheriff's Dept. spends countless man-hours, and in some cases, years, catching those responsible for everything from hard drugs to multiple felonies, and what happens? In many cases, the courts just let them go. Either probation or they dismiss the charges, knowing full well, they are guilty and proven as such. What deterrent is that? Then, the courts will turn around and sentence someone with possession of "one" joint of pot to years in jail. Something is just not right with our legal system.

If I were a deputy, I would be fed up. I would throw my hands up in disgust and walk out. They risk their lives every day to get crime off our streets, and out of our neighborhoods and for what? The courts just let them go. I know I am fed up, so I can imagine what it must be like for them.

There appears to be some "influence peddling" going on here. It sure is something. If they are going to let criminals go, don't waste taxpayer dollars taking them to court. Cut out taxes and overhaul the courts. They sure could use it.

May 15, 2005

Media General

I wrote to you in Jan. 04 about Letters to the Editor in the *Amherst New-Era Progress*. They were taking out any negative comments and questions I had in my letters. I am about the only citizen that sends letters to the paper asking questions or making a comment about our elected officials, that we as taxpayers should be able to do. I do not call names or say anything bad about anyone, but I still get edited.

You have a problem with someone in Amherst. And the reason I know that to be true is this. Your paper *The News and Advance*, in Lynchburg, publishers letters (2 enclosed) saying negative things all of the time. One man called the City Council, Jerry Falwell and the citizens of Lynchburg hypocrites. If I say anything like that in my letters, I get censored. If they can be published in one paper, they can be published in all. I have many negative letters from the Lynchburg paper, so I can prove my point.

This to me is discrimination. I am not saying your paper is doing this, but some "officials" are. The *Amherst New-Era Progress* in 1-04 even told me they could get sued, because of my letters. That is just not true.

First, I have not written letters the paper could get sued over. Someone out in Amherst has told them that. Second, the letters I write are my opinion, not the papers. Freedom of speech means nothing unless you can use it. Many citizens in the county tell me to keep writing my letters. They even want me to ask questions for them, because they are afraid too. I wonder why?

Your Amherst paper is excellent except for this problem of editing out the negative comments, questions or letters. The citizens should have the right to ask them, although, none have been answered. I have all of my letters, and when you compare them to the ones the paper publishes, you can see what they have taken out. I am sure you have the papers on file. The one thing I do know is this, someone more powerful than the paper is calling the shots in Amherst, or you have a close associate to some of them, on staff.

Without having the freedom to ask questions and voice your opinion in the paper, there is no way to let people know of things, that can and do, affect them. This should not be happening.

June 6, 2005

Marijuana

I think it is time to appoint "ordinary citizens" to the Supreme Court. The justices we have up there now need to use some logic. What are they thinking? Or are they? Why are they so determined to keep marijuana illegal? That will not stop its use. They may as well sit fire to Fort Knox, because that's the kind of tax money they are loosing. The tax dollars from the sale of marijuana would solve many of our money problems in this country. If you want tax relief, this is it. But no, the government just sits by and let the drug dealers have all the money.

Alcohol is legal and it kills. The drug called cigarettes is legal, and they kill. Prescription drugs are legal and they kill. Guns are legal and they kill. Need I go on? Marijuana is illegal and has killed no one. Where is the logic here? Marijuana use will never stop. Never, ever, ever.

People need to petition Congress to change the law on the use of marijuana. Many sick people will benefit from it. That is the most important thing. As it is now, a dying user will be carted off to jail, if caught. How pathetic. I do not use drugs, so either way it would not affect me, but God help those it could.

The intrusion into our lives by our so-called, "government" is becoming more Communist every day. You can't even sit on your own front porch, in view of a road, and drink a beer without going to jail. And people still call this a free country? When pigs fly!

Contributors to the paper should not be stopped from asking questions because someone's toes are being stepped on.

I hope someone can explain why this is happening. Someone, somewhere should be able to provide the answers.

July 9, 2005

Fireworks

July 4th is a time to celebrate our freedom, but many go to extremes. One such area is on Izaak Walton Road between Partridge Creek Road and Almay Drive near the new bridge. The fireworks and discharging firearms in this area has gotten way out of hand. There is at least one lady who is in her 80's who goes to bed at dark, but she was kept up half the night during this so called "celebration". Many of us have to work the holidays. It's hard to get any sleep when this goes on all night.

There are many dogs that are kept outdoors and they were howling and barking because they were scared to death. Starting July 3rd at 9 p.m. and continuing to 4 a.m., and on July 4th starting at 9 p.m. until 1 a.m., this area sounded like a war zone. Loud fireworks are bad enough, but when they are using firearms, you have no idea where they are aiming, especially under the influence of alcohol. It is ok to celebrate, but have a little respect for the neighbors and pets. Since some pay no attention to the fact that they are illegal and they are determined to shoot them off anyway, I offer this, get out in the yard in the daytime like a man, and not under the cover of darkness like the Ku Klux Klan.

The Board of Supervisors needs to pass an ordinance addressing this, now. The fines imposed on anything today are way to low. They are just a pat on the hand. Slap a five hundred dollar fine on anyone causing this kind of noise after dark. And if they are using firearms, take them and don't give them back. When there is a chance they will lose their precious firearms, it will stop. It is a shame some people have no respect for their neighbors and pets. But that is going to change.

The Klan name was left out for some reason. Must be some around.

July 20, 2005

Sign Ordinance

Some people in this county have a lot of nerve. In the July 14 issue of the Amherst paper, the article on the proposed sign ordinance struck me as funny at first, but them it made me downright mad. We have here a person or persons whining about the "cost" of complying with the proposed sign ordinance. Now, if I owned about everything along Route 29 North and half the county, I think I could come up with enough money to comply. It's real simple. Just sell an acre or two and that should take care of it. All of the other businesses with much less money will be complying.

What is so irritating is the fact that those doing the whining live in exclusive areas or subdivisions, in mansions, and they are saying they do not have the money to comply with a sign ordinance? If they have no money, then how do you get to live so "high on the hog"? Give me a break. They should be the first ones to step up and comply. Then, since they are so fortunate to own so much prime land, help the little businesses out. Any whining should come from the little businesses that are much less fortunate.

I don't think they will have to worry about keeping the big signs much longer. When the new bypass fully opens, they won't have that much traffic anyway. Take the big one's down and put up a few nice green one's along the bypass, advertising which exit to take to locate a certain business. And if Amherst County doesn't want to do that, then, it's a waste of time to even ask anyone to locate in the county. It sure works in other towns.

The way this thing is playing out so far lies in this fact. If you have money, you can stall anything. Or it could just be your pedigree. Amherst County can do better than this.

July 26, 2005

Mayors Son

I am an older white woman living in Amherst County. I have never met the Mayor or any of his family, but I do have an opinion, (which I am sure most will not give a hoot about), on the recent TV news media coverage of his son's court appearance.

The TV news was following him down the street, filming his back. This is not news, its harassment. Were they trying to get him to jump at them and tell them to get out of his face? Now that would have probably made their day! But that did not happen, did it?

You have doctors, lawyers, public officials, etc. whose children have been accused of any number of crimes. Where is the news media when they come to court? Were they hustled in and out a side door?

Remember, there are many "good" people who do bad things and this young man has not been convicted of anything yet, so give him a break. I think he handled himself like a perfect gentleman, and he came out the "front" door and walked down the sidewalk like a man. I applaud his parents for instilling that in him. I am proud of the way he handled himself. Even at my age, I do not think I could have done as well.

I fully expect to see on the TV news in the future, everyone's face that comes out the courthouse doors that has been accused of a crime. Trail them "all" down the street. Surely they do not want to discriminate.

This was published in the *The Lynchburg News and Advance*

September 23, 2005

Art Gallery

With increasing interest in this year's Art Show featured at the Library's Annual Book Sale, it's time for the county to help find or build a Art Gallery. The county spends money on the Coolwell Community Center, the kids sports fields, which were needed, a amphitheater, car racetrack, etc. Now it is time for a small art gallery. Build one onto the community center. No need for windows, just a door.

We art lovers have been denied use of the courthouse after using it for years, because we put holes in the walls. We offered to install the Walker System, used to hang art with no holes, but we were still refused. So, it wasn't really the holes that were the problem. That's one thing about Amherst County, you cannot get a straight answer from anyone.

Here we have a county that is home to the Virginia Center for the Creative Arts, which hosts renowned artist from all over the world, and no art gallery. That is a disgrace.

The Coolwell Community Center has parking and a good location. We art lovers have been ignored long enough. It's time for the county official's to get this ball rolling and think of us, because we pay taxes like everyone else.

And, to find the money, that would be simple. The public officials could cut out their trips and pork barrel spending. And if push comes to shove, give up your salaries for a year. Sitting in a chair and arguing one evening a month does not justify a salary. You should do that for nothing.

October 15, 2005

Art Gallery

In regard to a concern over tax increases from one reader for an art gallery in the county, I ask this. Were taxes raised for the Coolwell Community Center, the nature trails, the lakes up Route 60, the Industrial Parks, the Coolwell Convenience Center, to name a few? If so, I heard no complaints when they were built. Any tax increase for the remodeling of the old school on Phelps Road?

Why would anyone assume taxes would be raised for a one-room art gallery? No one is asking for the Empire State Building here.

There will be a room available in the old school building when remodeled and parking, or when they move half of the offices in Amherst down there, then there will be a room where they are now located. No need to raise any taxes. Just one empty former classroom or vacant room needed.

If you can build all the things we have built in this county without a big tax increase, why should one little room cause such a fuss? I am sorry to be the bearer of bad news, but taxes will be going up again and it will not be because of one little room. That's a given.

If you do for some, you should do for all. Artists pay their fair share of the taxes and all they are asking for is one little room to use, no more, no less.

November 22, 2005

Chavez

I find it interesting how the media is so determined to find fault with every person our government does not like, when they try to help the less fortunate. As crooked as some are in our government, I would not talk about anyone else. I have watched our government change for over 50 years. And their lies and shady deals "aren't pretty."

President Chavez of Venezuela is sending free oil to the needy in our country. Who cares if he is doing it for political gain? Who cares if he a friend of Fidel Castro? Who cares if he does not like Bush? Many of our taxpayers don't like him either. The important thing here is he is helping those who need oil for the winter.

Our government should accept all the help it can get. They can tell Chavez "Even though some in our government do not like you, we will gladly take your oil for the less fortunate, because we would rather throw our money away on a war that we will never win." There has been fighting in the Middle East since time began and there will still be fighting when it ends. We cannot be saviors of the world. This country needs to stay within its own borders and take care of its own.

If you would like to know, go on-line and read some foreign newspapers. Look at this country through their eyes. As far as the oil from Chavez, I say, "bring it on."

December 5, 2005

Amherst Game

In regard to the Amherst/Salem football game, I have a few comments. Here is another classic example of "legally stealing." I have seen many things in my life, but this "takes the cake." Who ever made up the rules for what is considered a touchdown and what is not, had better go back to the drawing board. Any play that was called wrong should be called back. I do not care if it's a month later. Do not decide the winner until it can be sorted out.

This is where camera's come into play. If the "rule makers" can't afford them, the money had better come from somewhere. This outcome is not acceptable, in no way, shape or form.

Some will say this is just a "game." Tell that to the kids who have worked their hearts out for years to become one of the best. Does anyone other than them know how much it hurts? Something like this would bring down an elephant.

How can the other team and their coaches live with themselves? When they saw the news footage, they should never have accepted the seven points. They knew they did not deserve them. What is this teaching the kids? Do some need to be the best so bad, that they take points they did not earn? Win at all cost must be what they were taught here. The other team did not deserve to be given the game, and say what you might; Amherst would have and did win that game.

Every parent, school, and officials involved in this mess should see that changes are made in the rules. Have cameras or no game. You cannot trust people. This is unacceptable. Hearts can mend, but what about spirits?

Chapter 7

2006

January 7, 2006

No Time Shares

A comment on time-shares, developers and officials. I do not live in Allwood, but I admire those who do for standing up for their community. The best thing developers can do is leave those people alone and let them live in peace in the "country." If they want to build time-shares, go to the beach. There are none here!!

The officials in the county view things like this: With more people comes more tax money, which provides more services. But, who wants more of either? Not Allwood and some other parts of the county. If you do want more, go somewhere else and don't push them down the throats of those who have made Amherst County their home all of their life. Amherst County has been "over developed" too much already. If you want to live "high on the hog," go to New York and give those who like the "country" a break.

The problem with Amherst County today is developers are buying up every inch of land they can get their hands on and putting a house on it. They do not care about anyone else, the land, or the wildlife. It's all about them and how much money they can make. They just plow right over anyone in their way and will continue to do so until the people of the county put a stop to it, by electing officials with more "common sense" than "book sense." It's been that way lately in Amherst County and it will continue until the people say "enough is enough." And, by the time that happens, it may be too late.

The county would have been well off today, if it hadn't been for our "officials." If they had allowed Busch Gardens to build here, the county would be sitting pretty and we would not need all of this "development." They shot themselves in the foot on that one. And Williamsburg got it all.

I plan to keep on speaking out about this "over development." Now if the "officials" do not like it, buy me a house with 100 acres of land back in the country and you will here nothing else from me. I give you permission to use "my tax dollars." But until them, I plan to keep on "keeping on." This is my New Year's resolution.

January 15, 2006

Another Ordinance

I did not give anyone in these United States my ok to restrict what I can or cannot do on my own property. People have always kept whatever they chose to on their land, and as long as the taxes are paid by the landowner, no one in this country should have anything to do with it.

The taxpayers are the majority and they are the ones who run this county. We pay the Board of Supervisors and others to take care of the county's expenses, and not to sit around thinking of ways to separate us from our money. Many taxpayers do not want the ordinance about "inoperable vehicles," as it has been proposed, and you must abide by our wishes because you work for us, and we are the majority. Only a "few" want to limit the rights of the majority.

"Inoperable vehicles," you say, are a fire hazard and hindrance in fighting fires, harbor rodents and insects, attractive nuisance to children, a health and safety hazard, detrimental to the citizens and reduce market value. You left out brush piles and old, vacant buildings, to name a few. They fit all of the above also.

On Izaak Walton Road are two lots that have been cleared to build houses. The builder has pushed up piles of trees as tall as a house, back behind where the house is going to be built. There is nothing more of a fire hazard than this and the builder has no intention of moving them. Case in point: Check out the bank behind the three new homes at the bottom of Dogwood Drive and Izaak Walton Road. More brush pushed down over the hill, and left by the same builder. Do you think Jerry Falwell knows this, as it borders the churches property?

If you fine vehicle owners, fine those with brush piles, and anyone who has old vacant buildings also. I fully expect them to be added to this ordinance, if not; you are prejudice against "just" vehicle owners. The "inoperable vehicle" is only the tip of the iceberg concerning this little problem.

February 20, 2006

Fire Department

Here we go again. Now the Amherst Fire Department is the target. Why should they hand over a key to a building they own? It does not belong to the local officials. And, why "hire" paid firefighters when there are those who care enough to do it for free. That is true dedication and that you cannot buy. This is just a "control" game.

If I am not mistaken, the land the Fire Department building sits on belongs to the taxpayers and not the Board of Supervisors, The Department of Public Safety or Emergency Services. And if so, the taxpayers should take it out of the Board of Supervisors hands and deed it to the Amherst Fire Department. That would solve this little problem.

Our local officials are sorely lacking in the way they are running the county. They have problems with the Humane Society, problems with the Pizza Hut, problems with time-shares, to name a few, and now the Amherst Fire Department. Problems, problems, and problems. The one thing they seem to have gotten right so far is the Coolwell Dump.

Let the taxpayers decide. I support the volunteers. They are part of our country's heritage.

March 18, 2006

Accident

I would like to thank everyone who offered assistance to my son at the accident on Route 130/Elon Road, Sunday, March 12, involving a motorcycle and a truck. We both cannot thank you enough. It is a miracle he survived.

What makes this serious accident even worse is that, the person who pulled out in front of him kept going. You do not leave an injured animal lying in the highway, much less a human being. And, my son had taken a new job and had not been there long enough for medical insurance. It is a shame there are still people around who put such little value on human life. But, what goes around comes around. Thank you again to everyone who offered their help. It was greatly appreciated.

March 20, 2006

Confusing Decisions

I have lived in this county 65 years and have seen many changes. Do the things listed below show that the board is dedicated and concerned about the welfare of the county? These are some of the things that create lots of questions and no answers, so far.

Changing the county seal without the consent of the taxpayers, passing zoning laws without public input, purchasing a farm never listed for sale to expand the Amelon Park without informing the taxpayers, refusing Applebee's Restaurant a permit to build where the new BB&T now sits, refusing permits for restaurants next to Lowe's, and someone removed court cost and fines from the newspaper when asked where all of that money went, etc.

I will support our county officials when they make good decisions and explain them to the taxpayers. All we get now are closed-door meetings where they can get around the taxpayers.

As for electing a new board, we already have one person in the county that has more "common sense" than all of us out together. He is the answer to this county's problems. Not because of any affiliation with a political party, but because he is totally educated about everything he speaks about. The supervisors only see what they want to see, but Steven C. Martin sees it all, and he is totally right on the money. So if you want to get this county moving in the right direction, turn it over to him. Someone like him only comes along once in a lifetime. He is an incredibly wise and astute man and would be a godsend to Amherst County, if the taxpayers would elect him to office. He will listen to you and he would "hear" what you have to say.

March 31, 2006

Seek Office

I have a sure fire way of turning Amherst County around and putting it on the fast track to becoming one of the nicest places in the state. I have been reading the Letters to the Editor in both the *Amherst New-Era Progress* and the *Lynchburg News and Advance* for sometime. We have among us a person whose letters I have read on many issues and have been amazed as to how well informed he is on anything he speaks out about. I like him, not because he is affiliated with any certain political party, but because he is "right on the money" about what he has to say. A real "common sense" type of guy whom I do not know personally.

We need "common sense" to precede an educated mind, but that is not happening with the Board of Supervisors today. We also need to set term limits. You cannot get new ideas when the same people control the county from year to year and see their "hand picks" get elected. The voters need to know their views before putting them in office and hold them to what they promise. When they make these decisions the majority do not like, kick them out immediately and put someone in their place. Each supervisor should have their own web site and talk about their views and answer questions from the taxpayers. Some taxpayers cannot make the meetings and this is one way they could get involved. Right supervisors?

So if you want Amherst County to prosper, put someone with "common sense" into a position to do good for all of us. Talk Stephen C. Martin into taking over the reins and running this county. He is wiser than every county official put together. The only place we have to go is "up."

May 21, 2006

Speeders, etc

There are a couple of problems in Amherst County that need addressing. One is the road going to the Coolwell Convenience Center. Many patrons of the dump are annoyed with the potholes, but they need to address the county officials and not the nice man who works there. If the county cannot repair them, then they should pay to have those affected, with "free" alignments.

The other problem is to get these "speeders" under control. And, they are older people and not teenagers. 90% of those traveling Izaak Walton Road try to run over you. There is no sense in "grown" people speeding and endangering children, animals or any poor person who happens to be in their way. They pass you on a double line even if you are going 5 mph over the speed limit. It has got to stop.

I think most drivers can read, but the speed limit between Amelon United Methodist Church and Sheetz, may as well say 65 mph instead of 35. Why post a speed limit if you cannot enforce it?

This is where cameras and huge fines come into play. There are three ways to handle this problem. One is to place cameras to clock drivers and send them a ticket. Pretty soon, the cameras would be paid for. Second, put cobblestone down over the asphalt. That will surely work. Or the best of all, a mandatory $500.00 fine for the first speeding ticket, and you loose you license for a year, for the second one. Then you would see them come to a screeching halt.

Something needs to be done for those who drive responsibility, in order for them to live a little longer. And, it needs to be done now, not after they are dead.

May 29, 2006

Rentals

I have a few comments on the article about rentals. First, government officials have been telling us how we can use our land for years. And, as far as the Board of Supervisors goes, I think they were referring to "future" development of vacation rentals, not one's private land.

You cannot preserve what's left of Amherst County until you get control of development. Only those after more money want to put up "vacation" rentals in every little spot they can find. I would like them to explain to everyone, where the wildlife is going to go, where are we going to raise the food we and the livestock eat, and how are people going to have a quiet community when all of the vacation rentals go up?

Now if they want to go to the mountains, there is always the Pocono's. We do not want to turn Amherst County into that. We like the quiet "laid back" communities we have now, what few we have left. We would not need more income in the county if we keep it simple, stop the destruction of our land, and "vacation rentals" go elsewhere. More development means more automobiles, etc. and a good chance of drug dealers taking advantage of the rentals to deal their drugs, and move on to the next town. You never really know whom you are renting too. You cannot search every person who rents the property.

What we have here are people who want to turn this county into a resort, of sorts, and those who have lived here all their life, who want peace and quiet. So, I offer this suggestion. Create a conservation easement /land trust. You can still sell your land or leave it to your heirs, but the restrictions you place on it, go with the sale. Look into it. It guarantees the land will not be developed "forever and a day." "There is more than one way to skin a cat"!

June 10, 2006

Radar Cameras

I do support more law enforcement and I did complain about the stop sign incident, but I would have done that for anyone. It just happened to be my son who was stopped, and that is how I became aware of this area. I also classify "real" criminals, as murderers, robbers, drug dealers etc. I do not think someone who looks and then proceeds through a stop sign is a criminal. I have followed a school bus that did the same thing. It's nothing new. My point was there should have been a yield sign there, given the circumstances.

Automated cameras designed to catch speeders would put a stop to stereotyping or profiling. The camera system does not care what color you are or what type of car you drive; if you are speeding, you are busted. They would also provide income for deputy's salaries, and free up police to catch "real" criminals. I am all for hiring a deputy for every square mile of Amherst County, but gee, no money! Unless you up speeding fines and use other legal means to obtain more income for salaries, you will never get a handle of speeders or criminals. There are just not enough deputies; so bring on the cameras. I give permission for my tax dollars to be used for them.

Camera footage is used in court every day. Ever heard of them being in police cars? What about surveillance cameras? Even Uncle Sam can pick out our license plate from a satellite; so no sane person is going to get up in court and challenge a picture, because a picture is worth a thousand words. Cameras will work all right. And as for having the "right" to be confronted by an officer or having my rights violated, poppycock! But, what do I know?

June 28, 2006

Upholding Wrong

I cannot for the life of me understand some people. When parents bring children into this world they are suppose to teach them right from wrong. You are supposed to praise them for the good things they do, and punish them for the bad. So why would anyone whose child has caused an accident and left someone laying in the highway to die, ruffle their feathers at the person their child almost killed?

I must be poured from a different mold than most, because if my son had caused that accident, I would personally escort him to jail, and tell him that he is responsible for his actions, and as such, stand up like a man and take his punishment. I would not aid his fleeing the state. What kind of love and support is that? Sounds more like "accessory after the fact," to me.

I did not go to court with my son the other day, because if I had, I would probably be keeping company with the inmates in the county jail, and not sitting in the comfort of my home, writing this letter. It is only natural to be upset when your child has becomes a victim, and I was raised around "banny roosters," so that court day was my cooling off period. But, later this year, I will be there.

How can anyone justify leaving an injured person lying in the highway? There are some people in this world that just have no compassion for their fellow human beings. Such a sad waste of their lives.

July 12, 2006

Art Show

I would like to personally thank Rebecca Massie Lane and Sweet Briar College for the honor of inviting the Amherst Art Society to hold its recent show in the Pannell Gallery. It is nice to know someone in the county appreciates our work. That is more than I can say for some of our county officials. We can hang art in the Nelson County Court House but not in the Amherst County Court House. Go figure!

A prestigious college has noticed us and that is very empowering. Many in the state have also recognized us. We are not going to disappear into the sunset, but are moving "full steam" ahead. It is time for the county to jump on board this fast moving train.

Our annual art show will be held on Saturday, September 9, from 8 am to 2 pm. in cooperation with the Friends of the Amherst Library Book and Bake Sale. This is an open invitation to the young artist in our schools. Our young people are our future, so come join us.

Please come by the Amherst Library and see what we are all about; buy as book, baked goods, a work of art, and enjoy lunch from our vendor. Please support our effort to bring the appreciation for art back to the "front and center" in Amherst County.

August 12, 2006

Freedom of Speech

The letter in your August 9th issue of the *Lynchburg News and Advance* from Mr. Hovda shows me I am not alone, in what we have to deal with while trying to exercise "free speech." I have had this same problem since 1999 in writing my Letter's to the Editor. I give my opinion on officials and issues that should be addressed. If someone does not like what I am saying about an issue or person, they cut it out. This goes on in 90 percent of my letters.

The 1st Amendment gives us the right to "free speech." If we cannot exercise this right in the newspaper, where do we exercise it? No one should be able to interfere with this right when it is done in a reasonable way. That is the law.

Public officials should be accountable to the people, and the newspaper should be our platform in which to address them, in our own words, and not a "watered down version." If they can't stand the heat, get out of the kitchen. The news media or their acquaintances should not have the power to change someone's letters to suit them.

The *Amherst New-Era Progress* is also bad about his. Those who talk to me about the letters I write know about all of the censorship that is going on. So the public knows, in a lot of cases, they are only getting half of the story. I would expect this if we lived in a Communist country, or is that already the case?

August 24, 2006

Railway Trail

I have some comments on the article about the Railway Trail. What is with the difference in fencing? If you put boards and wire mesh on one person's property, put it on everyone's. With the new fees for special exemptions going up from $25 to $300, you sure can afford it.

Anytime a project affects someone else's land, the landowners should be consulted. That would be the case here, if the county does not have a deed. I see no one threatening the county, but people are fed up with some of the county officials because of their overbearing ways.

And as for the comment, "I have nothing better to do than keep the county tied up in court"; you go Mr. Janetatoes! If more people would stand up, speak out, and back it up with action, this would be the best county in the state.

Finally, anyone whose blood pressure is going up over this, I offer this advice. Your health is one the line, so take some time off or retire. Mr. Janetatoes would make a great replacement!

This letter was not published for whatever reason.

August 24, 2006

Error

Please inform your readers about the error you made regarding my letter in this week's paper. I said "There are **not** enough deputies to sit along it with a radar gun, so it's time to get hold of a camera." You left out the word **not**, which changed the entire sentence. So if anyone sends in a response, let them know it was an error on your part. You need to proof read the letters after retyping to make sure they are accurate. Mistake's like this is not responsible journalism.

September 9, 2006

Art Show Parking

I have a few things to say concerning the town police. The morning of the Art Show a few artist were parked behind the library on Kenmore Road to unload their artwork. And because they had two tires on the pavement, this was deemed illegal, so they had to move immediately. No one was blocking the road, and some were older and could not drag boxes from the parking lot of the church up the hill, down to the lawn.

The same officer then spent most of his day running back and forth, writing tickets and placing them on cars parked along Kenmore Road. As fast as one would leave, he would be back to ticket some other poor soul. He mentioned to someone, that Kenmore Road was an intersection. But so is every other side street in Amherst. They intersect with the main road. Dah! He also stated he had placed cones along part of the road, but ran out. So, given that, it was the town's fault, not the people parking there. No one in going to park illegally and risk getting a ticket just to view artwork.

How are the people supposed to know? They do not have a codebook. The state should provide one to every citizen, but the reason they do not is simple. Then, everyone would find out about the other sneaky codes they know nothing about, cause an uproar and they would risk losing those fines.

Many people work hard to build up the arts here in the county and this year we almost doubled in exhibitors. But the customers won't be coming back after they get a ticket they did not deserve. This is incompetence on the part of town officials, not the people who attended the show. Take all of the prior fines and buy some more cones. And while they are at it, tear up the ones they wrote Saturday. If the state cannot find a way to let the people know about all of the codes, take them off the books. Those people were taken advantage of. This was a case of entrapment, plain and simple.

September 13, 2006

Freedom of Speech?

Media General, Inc.

I wrote to you back in Jan. 04 about the *Lynchburg News and Advance* and the *Amherst New-Era Progress*. I have been writing letters for years that have been edited and/or not published, and I can't understand why. I know the papers have a right to edit things, but if you say nothing in your letter to cause a lawsuit, why cut it out? Every time there is a sentence someone does not like they just take it out. I have many letters that have been edited and those I have showed them to, do not see anything that should cause their removal. I am sending you three of them. One is from a man they did publish (Aug.9,) and the one I sent to the *Lynchburg News* (Aug.12) they would not publish. Why not? Also, I am including one I sent to the *Amherst New-Era Progress* (Aug. 24) they would not publish. I see nothing wrong with these letters. If you write unfavorably about any official in Amherst, they will not publish it. That is not right.

My Aug.12 letter explains what I mean. I think anytime a letter has been edited, the writer has a right to know why. You cannot get a straight answer from those who do not like you for whatever reason. For some reason, when you speak out, you are stopped in your tracks by these two papers. Some so called "freedom of speech." Maybe you can explain why all this censorship is happening. People have told me they will not write letters to the paper because they are edited so much. People should be able to speak out in their own words and feel they will be heard.

This sounds more like what the U.S. Government would do, rather than of a newspaper. Freedom of Speech is important and a necessity, but some do not have it in the media when we need it most. They pick and chose who can be criticized and whom they will publish. If you step on somebody's toes, you're out. I know you are a busy person, but maybe you can give me an honest answer. The "little people" out here needs some help.

October 3, 2006

Editor

I cannot reach you by phone during the day, as I am working or in class. So I will send you this letter by fax. I appreciate you printing my letters, but I am trying to figure out why some are not printed. That is why I wrote to Media General. Maybe they would tell me the difference between the two letters I mention below.

I am aware of your policy, but that did not answer the question as to why some of my letters were not published.

The letter dated August 24th about the Railway Trail was one example. There were no personal attacks and nothing said to get the newspaper sued. So why was it not published?

Some of the county officials are overbearing and the citizens should have the right to voice their opinion on their behavior. They are supposed to answer to us because we pay their salary. Anytime I say something that looks negatively on a county official, it is not published. I don't think they own the newspaper.

As for accuracy, how can you possibly check all of the letters you publish for accuracy? No one has ever called me from the paper to discuss the accuracy of mine. I would also like for you to point out to me where I have attacked someone or put the newspaper in danger of being sued.

As for the letter dated August 12 to the *Lynchburg News and Advance*, there was nothing wrong with that letter, except it showed they pick and choose who they will publish. Mr. Horvda's letter was much more brazen than mine and it was published. So what happened there? Read the letter from me (Aug 12) and from Mr. Hovda (Aug 9) to the *Lynchburg News and Advance*. Compare the two and tell me as a journalist, where my letter shows personal attack or libel. That is the question I am trying to get answered.

I am just trying to figure out what the difference was in these two letters where one could be published and the other couldn't. If there isn't any libel issue or personal attacks, then there has to be another reason, and the only thing left would be the writer. You will not get a straight answer from the *Lynchburg News and Advance.*

You have published letters far worse than those I write. If the *Lynchburg News* hasn't been sued by Jerry Falwell, by now, they never will be sued. He is attacked every day. I do not attack anyone personally, so go through my letters and show me which one's show libel and personal attacks.

I understand you have the right not publish letters, but I think the writer should know the reason they were not published, or the reason they were edited. No perfect English should be needed, just a person's own words. We the readers keep the newspaper in business. Thanks for the ones you do publish.

November 20, 2006

Dump

Someone from the county needs to get up out of their chair and go down and repair the potholes going into the Coolwell Convenience Center dump. There are potholes that need fixing and with the taxes you collect, there is no sense in putting up with those potholes. You can go down to Lowes, buy some bags of asphalt repair for $9.98 plus tax, for a 50 lb. bag. That would take about all of $70.00 to repair those potholes. And if you cannot afford to hire people to do the work, I am sure the inmates at the County Jail would be glad to help out.

You are considering developing every inch of the county and you cannot keep up with the repairs you already have. If you cannot keep up with them, don't bring any more developments in here to make them worse. You think traffic was bad before the by-pass opened? Just wait until you see the traffic from the River Road development. The only thing missing now are the trucks. It is still awful and getting worse every day. Where is all the money going that these new houses are paying in taxes? It sure isn't going to repair roads.

Given all that, this is what is going to happen. Either someone is going down there and fix those potholes or my husband and I are going to call an independent contractor, have him repair the potholes, and send the bill to the Board of Supervisors. They say people have more patience when they age, but mine has just about run out. There is no sense in letting a county facility get in such disrepair.

Oh, also send a locksmith down there and have him remove the key that broke off in the compactor months ago. The taxpayer deserve better, because we bought them in the first place. The least the county can do is keep them and the road up.

December 21, 2006

Jail

In regard to this jail issue, I offer this suggestion. Since we the taxpayers will have to foot part of the bill, it should be up to all of the taxpayers to decide whether they want the jail here, and not the Board of Supervisors.

The board cannot represent everyone in the county, without dialog. Given that, the taxpayers should flood the Board of Supervisors and anyone else connected to this issue with emails. If they do not have the time to read them and respond, they are in the wrong job. Bring on those who will listen and vote with the majority.

People need to voice their opinion. Go to the county web site and you will find their email addresses. This is the perfect way for those who cannot attend the meetings to have a say. Let the majority decide, since it will affect us all.

As far as finding the perfect piece of property goes, surely those real estate developers who are destroying the rest of the county, would be glad to find a site in the middle of nowhere for the jail to be built. Wouldn't you think?

Chapter 8

2007

January 4, 2007

Rebuttal

This is in regard to Wendy Nash's comments about the new jail.

What Mrs. Nash doesn't seem to understand is that no one wants a jail in their county. So what makes us so special that we would be exempt from this project?

Jails, landfills and other unsightly projects are part of every landscape, and something we must deal with. If we, as taxpayers, got to take a vote on these things, then there would be no jails anywhere and criminals would run free.

Jeff Quarles
Amherst

January 5, 2007

Jail

In response to Mr. Quarles letter, I need to clear up another misunderstanding. I did not say the jail could not be built in Amherst County. I said to put in "the middle of nowhere." I am sure some of the county officials have a hundred acres of their land they could sell and locate the jail there.

Also, our legal system needs refining. Put the non-violent offenders out and make them wear "prison garb" (colors of the courts choosing) with their offense written on it 24-7, for a year or however long. Plaster their faces everywhere, get them a job and take the money they earn for restitution and you will see a drop in the non-violent crime rate real quick. What you have now sure isn't working. Then you would have plenty of room in the jails you already have for the violent offenders. I am sure there are some very bright people out there who could come up with a workable plan and I don't need to hear that this will not work, because I know better.

But, just go ahead and put the jail in a populated area and you will be out of a job come re-election. People are fed up. There is plenty of underdeveloped land out there. It is your job to find it. That is what the taxpayers pay you for.

And finally, if I am still alive when the elections are held, I may just give it a shot. If I make it, I may not make a difference, but I sure will be a thorn in a lot of people's sides.

January 11, 2007

What Would the Unheard Say?

This responds to Jeff Quarles' rebuttal to Wendy Nash regarding the proposed new jail.

As published weekly, Amherst County residents, including myself, take great pride in voicing their opinion. I understand, and agree with much of Wendy Nash's letter two weeks ago. I understand, and agree with Mr. Quarles' practical view that no one wants a jail or other "unsightly projects" in their county. I also don't feel Amherst is considering everyone in the county.

As I read numerous letters pro and con for this new jail, I think a census of county residents, whose inaudible opinion of this proposed jail has been largely overlooked.

What about the folks at Central Virginia Training Center? Our voices are heard, but what about the individuals who live there? Wouldn't this jail affect them, just as we feel it would us? Of all the available land sites in the county, I feel it blatantly rude that the county's first choice is so close to a group of residents who may not be able to voice their concerns. Let's put the new jail beside the "colony". Let's put the inmates beside another group of folks society has historically looked away from. Put it on their backyard. We may argue a landfill or jail in <u>our</u> neighborhood, but is not the site off Virginia 210 <u>their</u> neighborhood? Who hears them? I daresay if the proposed jail site was beside Hans Hill, the uproar would be deafening.

Beth Franklin
Madison Heights

January 12, 2007

Speak Out

It sure is nice to see the taxpayers beginning to stand up and speak out. Thank you to Ms. Franklin and Mr. Wood. And, I must say, Mr. Wood, I love you. You are a real supervisor. Please do run again and I just may join you, because I have been fed up long enough. I hope all who speaking out will consider running.

This is what a supervisor's job is supposed to be. You are elected to look out for the taxpayers in the district you represent. They hire you to vote their views, not your own. That is where mistakes are made. You must represent your district and not the entire county, good or bad. If that was how it should be, only one supervisor would have a job. Publish your email address and phone number and let the taxpayers tell how they want you to vote. If you vote yes or no on every issue, so be it. It should be your district's call.

I agree with Mr. Wood. You must elect people who will listen to those they represent. If you don't, the taxpayers should have the power to remove you from office anytime and replace you will someone else. If they put you in, they can take you out. No term limits on misrepresentation. There may be hope for the county yet. The ball is finally rolling, so some had better watch out!

March 21, 2007

Rings

I have a few things to say about the state championship rings, a little late, but nevertheless here it is. The questions raised with regard to this issue were from concerned adults.

I would like to know why anyone should expect those young athletes to pay for their own rings. This happened to be a state championship game and the state should be the ones to pay for the rings. These kids worked their tails off for this county and the state, and put them both on the map.

Think about all the money that was taken in. The county took in a lot of money from all of the Amherst games. Did they spend it all to rent the stadium at Liberty or was that free? You know someone made a bundle of money on that game.

The way I see it is this; we pay state income taxes and our tax dollars are going to support the schools. Since this was a school championship game, the state should pay at least ¾ of the cost of the rings, because the state hands out the money for the schools, and the county could pay the rest. It's nice that other people wanted to contribute, but it was not their responsibility to pay for the rings either.

I do not care how many state championship games they have, in whatever sport, the bottom line is this. If it is a state championship game, the state buys the winner's rings. Our tax dollars pay for everything else, so to speak, so why not the rings? The county and state get all the glory, the money raised, and the kids get nothing? This is totally absurd. Something is wrong here.

It is not the winner's responsibility to be running around selling things to make money to pay for rings they already won. They won the game; they won the rings. If you win something, it is yours. You do not pay for it.

There are way too many of our tax dollars being wasted on stupid stuff. At least with a ring, we can see where our money went. The county and the state should do better by our kids. They are not panhandlers or beggars; they are state championship winners and should be treated as such. This issue is not over by a long shot.

March 27, 2007

What Am I All About

For those who do not know me and wonder what I am all about, here's your chance to find out. The Senior Art Show of 2007 at Sweet Briar College will have its opening reception Friday, April 13, from 5-7 p.m. in the Pannell Gallery at Sweet Briar College, so mark your calendars.

I would like to invite the entire county and everyone else to drop by opening night. I think you will be pleasantly surprised. If you can't make Friday, the show will run through May 12th. Gallery hours will be 1 to 5 p.m. Sunday, Monday and Friday, 1 to 9:30 p.m. Tuesday, Wednesday and Thursday.

I support the preservation of the past, because when it is gone we can never get it back, and its importance is reflected in my work. I am also against over development, which is what we are faced with in the county now. There are better ways for the county to make money. Try some professional golf tournaments for one, and if you would turn the town of Amherst into a mini-Williamsburg, tourism would keep the county alive. Amherst sure could use a cobblestone Main Street. It would keep speed down without the help of law enforcement and it would be a pleasure to look at. Enough asphalt jungle!

We cannot keep putting up subdivisions on every square inch of land that is left. By promoting tourism, and getting people in here to spend their money, we are selling out our children. What "land" will they have if this keeps on? "If there is a will, there is a way." So, bring on the big money makers and remember there is no such word as "can't." Hope to see you at the opening!

Paper did not publish this letter for whatever reason. Must have been considered an advertisement.

May 8, 2007

Developers

Things to consider before opposing the Comprehensive Plan: What do developers, most real estate agents and some large land owners have in common? Money! Money! And more money!

1. Worried about additional tax burdens? Don't. They're coming anyway.

2. Worried about property rights? Where have these people concerned about this been living all these years? We lost most of those a long time ago.

3. If you do not have the money to move into a "Hans Hill," people will always be segregated, money wise. It's always been like that, you live where you can afford to.

If large landowners cared about their land, they would put it in a "land conservation easement" to protect it. Instead they sell to developers. Developers use the excuse that our property rights are in danger just to "stir people up." They aren't fooling me. It's all about money, not our property rights. Don't be fooled into thinking it is anything else.

If the Board of Supervisors mess this plan up, impeach them. If we can impeach a President, we sure can impeach a Board of Supervisors. Put people in office who care more about the land than money. Back the Comprehensive Plan so our kids can enjoy what's left of our county instead of living in an asphalt jungle.

June 1, 2007

Running for Office

A few things to consider before the election:

First, anyone serving on, or running for, the Board of Supervisors should live in the county. They should live among those they represent and then they would be better qualified to represent their interest.

Second, real estate agents, developers, etc. should not be on the Board of Supervisors, because then they could control anything having to do with land in this county, buy, sell, trade or take. This could be a disaster to land owners. Does this not cause a conflict of interest? They would be serving two masters here, themselves and the board members, not the taxpayers. You can bet most live on large amounts of land in fine homes, so what do they care? Anything to do with the comprehensive plan would not affect them. How many live on an acre of land next to you? We need our supervisors representing the citizens of Amherst County.

We really do not own our land anyway. If we do not keep up our taxes, they take it. That is what happened to the Monacan Indians. They were really poor in those days, so where were they going to get the money from? They wanted their land so they took it. If they don't get the land that way they declare eminent domain. If you are forced to sell, you never really owned your land anyway. We need people in office who will think of others rights before intruding upon their land.

As for right-of-ways, the county once had a school on a property owners land. Years after the school was gone, the land was deeded to the landowners where the school once stood. This should be the case with the trail. When the railroad tracks were abandoned, the land should have been deeded to the landowners. It was a right of way for a railroad and not a trail. This is totally not right.

So you see, nothing is really yours. They will get you coming and going. And when elections roll around be very cautious. "Be careful what you wish for."

June 13, 2007

Parking Meters

As if the county of Amherst hasn't been messed up enough, now they are trying to ruin the little town of Amherst. Why would anyone want to remove the vintage parking meters and replace them with new modern ones? Where does common sense come into this equation? What little money the new ones would generate is only a drop in the bucket. The old ones are part of the charm of the town of Amherst. Amherst should stay "vintage" and not be turned into a "state of the art" city of the future.

If you need money so bad, have more "street parties," but stop messing with the little town of Amherst unless you want to turn it into a mini Williamsburg.

June 20, 2007

Comprehensive Plan

In regard to the petition the developers had at the June 11 meeting, you can bet your bottom dollar the people who signed it do not have the whole story. They are only told what will scare them into signing the petition. People; please get both sides before you sign your life away.

As for the "carpetbaggers" remark, I would like to inform one attending the meeting, how disrespectful he was to people who know first hand what it is to live in an "asphalt jungle." We need more people like them in Amherst County, not developers. I also beg to differ with him on the reference that most people in this county are not vocal; because I am so vocal I make up about half of them.

And if I trusted the elected officials to "do the right thing," I would keep my mouth shut. People in the county will stand up for their dogs and their guns, but most are not standing up for our historic farmland and forest. Once the developers get their hands on the farms, etc. and develop them, they're gone forever.

The majority rules and that means the whole county, not just a few names on a petition. All citizens should have a say after they are informed on both sides on this issue. It's up to the board to figure out how because it will affect us all. What is the rush on this comprehensive plan if it isn't money? Put it on the ballot in November. The land isn't going anywhere.

July 15, 2007

Subdivisions

A few comments on the proposed subdivision to be built on Izaak Walton Road.

First, people who will be living in the lowest part should be made aware of the fact they will be sitting on the receiving end of sewage fields during heavy rains. Subdivision with 32 homes with low areas should be required to use a water treatment facility, and if there is none, don't build the homes. There should also be a clause in the sale agreement that states, "if problem's arise, the builder and/or county can be sued." If they can't do something right the first time, they should pay the second time. Most homeowners are usually at the mercy of the developers, builders and the county for allowing it to happen.

Second, with a hundred or so new cars on the road, will Izaak Walton get four lanes? It's used as a speedway now, because very few can read a speed limit sign. If they are impatient now, imagine what it will be like when the subdivision is up and running with a couple of hundred new cars racing down the road. Lord, help the school buses. There is always that great traffic camera just waiting to be installed that would bring in more money than taxes.

But wait, a camera doesn't have pockets to stuff. The one saving grace may be that the elections are coming. Maybe a change in the Board of Supervisors will help, but I wouldn't hold my breath. We have some voters who just have the knack of electing the wrong people.

Dump

A word of warning to the taxpayers of Amherst County. I understand the Board of Supervisors is planning to join a Regional Landfill with Nelson County, City of Bedford, City of Lynchburg and Campbell County. A joint effort is fine, but what's in the fine print is not. The Authority should not have total control over where and when the various landfills should be located and used. That should be up to each county to decide after consulting the taxpayers of that county.

The land in the county belongs to the taxpayers and not the region. The Authority would have the right to bring in trash from places like New York, New Jersey, etc., pollute our land, and the county could do nothing about it. We would have only one vote out of five. When you join, you loose the right to control your own landfill, for over 50 years. That is only the tip of the iceberg. Next it will be our water and sewage rights.

Do they need money bad enough to turn the county into a toxic waste dump? If they think this is going to wash, they have another think coming. The county has already been sold out to developers. Now they want to make it the trash capital of the world. Do they have any idea what they are doing??? It's time to get an incinerator. And I do not care how much they cost. Enough tax money has been wasted to pay for more than one. Amherst County is not the dumping ground for the rest of the world.

These so-called notices about the meetings put in the paper are so small I cannot read them with glasses on. They could at least make them big enough for the taxpayers to read. After all, it's our money they are using to have them printed. But that's the whole point of them being small. People wake up and let the Supervisors know how you feel before we get sold out again. Read all about it on the county website. Your life may depend on it. Sludge could be coming and, oh yes, plastic liners leak, with the help of medical waste and anything sharp, some protection there!

August 15, 2007

Experienced Candidates?

I cannot for the life of me figure out these ill-advised people claiming intelligence, trying to scare people into voting for a so-called "experienced candidate" for President. How dumb do they think people are? Take for example the constant jabs at Barack Obama. Whether you are for or against him is immaterial. The plain truth is an ordinary person off the street would make a better President than a politician controlled by money and special interest. We need someone who hasn't been corrupted yet, and as far as I can see, Obama is the only one in either party. There is nothing wrong with experience, but it's not that important. This is why. We have the Secretary of State, the Interior, Agriculture, Commerce, Justice, Defense, Labor, Education, Energy, Transportation, Health and Human Services and the Treasury. Now, tell me why the President needs experience? The Cabinet is there to advise and then a decision is made.

Anyone with "common sense" can listen to the facts and make the appropriate decision. So far "experience" has gotten us into a world of trouble. So enough with the "experienced candidate" baloney. We need someone who will end the war and save what's left of our youth, and build that fence on the Mexican border. Any candidate who is not for these two things will not get my vote.

For the record, I am an Independent.

September 15, 2007

Developments

I understand the county keeps okaying developments because they will bring in more money for the county, and will keep taxes lower. That is totally impossible. How can that be when you will have to spend every dime taken in and still raise out taxes to compensate, when you run out of money. Developments are not the answer to the counties problems. They are the cause of the problems we now have. And here is why.

Developments mean more road's, more road upkeep, more water lines, more sewage lines, more dumps, more dump trucks, higher garbage bills, higher water bills, more fire departments, more rescue squads, more jails, more schools, more school buses, more teachers, just to name a few. It's always more and more and more.

So keep on putting up houses on every acre of land in the county. If you think taxes are high now, just wait.

We do not need more businesses either. People move here to get away from all of that mumbo jumbo. They want to live in rural areas. If they had wanted to live in congestion, they would have settled in Lynchburg. Where has common sense gone? The answer to the county's problems is to stop the developing and take care of what you already have. Enough is enough.

If you do not use your right to speak out, one day soon, you will have no rights left. I have been around long enough to see where things are headed and it sure is not in the right direction. People think it will not make a difference if they speak up, but they are wrong. "For evil to win, good men must keep quiet" and unfortunately that is what the majority in the county are doing. Using common sense is the answer to our problems, not developments. Keep that in mind come election day.

October 24, 2007

Elections

Oh the tangled webs we weave. "Walk into my parlor said the spider to the fly." That is what is happening in Amherst County with the upcoming elections. The developers have engulfed this entire county with deceit. They weave their webs with money, instead of silk. It's a whole lot stronger and it causes the destruction of our environment. Money is the "root of all evil" and those who worship it, sell their souls to the devil. How do some have the nerve to show up for church on Sunday morning? God knows what is in their souls. They are not fooling him.

And some wonder what is behind the destruction of our planet, with the floods and fires, etc? Good ole greed. The Lord gave it to us and the way we are destroying it, he is going to take it away. Wake up people. You can change the destruction of our county come election day. God did not create the environment to be destroyed by man. Vote for the candidates who will save what is left of our county. Vote against the developers.

"Look deep into nature and then you will understand everything better," Albert Einstein

November 9, 2007

Elections

Reflecting on this year's elections, I have a few comments. Congratulations to Chris Adams and Don Kidd on being elected to the Board of Supervisors. It is reassuring to elect people that really care about what we have left of our rural areas, and controlling the counties growth. I am glad to see people standing up and speaking out on this important issue. And they did it where it counted most, at the polling booths.

As to those county officials who think they can still smother its taxpayers with developments, well, they had better think again. Your jobs will be next. People are not going to stand for it any longer. No more hiding behind closed doors. We are winning this war, one job at a time. So keep that in mine the next time you vote on an issue that goes against the majority of those you represent.

Also, thanks to the Amherst County taxpayers who made it happen. There may be a light at the end of this tunnel yet. "United we stand, divided we fall"

November 27, 2007

Assessments

Have the county officials completely lost their minds? These so-called tax appraisals are out of "this" world. How do they think people are going to pay these absurd taxes? Our income does not rise with tax increases or prices. We are not living in Hollywood.

Put some more of the "common sense" taxpayers in office and you will see a change. When do the others come up for re-election? We cannot take another four years of this. Instead of raising our taxes to this outrageous amount, bring some moneymakers into the county.

Use your heads for a change. Build a NASCAR track here. There sure is enough land and what noise it would make would not bother me half as much as standing in that welfare line. It would bring in more money in one year than they could make in ten. The only other thing to do is to go pick up your food stamps and welfare checks.

The people in the county had better come together and figure this out. Those in office as of this year sure are not doing anything but putting us out in the street. This is our county and it is time to take it back, in a peaceful manner. Give the "common sense," ordinary citizens a chance to show what they can do. "We the people, in order to form a more perfect union, have the power so says the Constitution, not the 'weasels in the chicken house." Looks like I may be heading to Social Services along with everyone else to pick up my food stamps. But!!! Not without a fight first.

December 1, 2007

Alert

As a taxpayer I would like to know why the current Board of Supervisors is trying to hire a lawyer "before" the new members take office. The voters of Amherst County duly elected the new supervisors, and as such, they have a right to be included in the hiring of any lawyer. If one is hired before January, and they are not part of the process, he is not representing them. What are those now in office trying to pull? It is not above board, or else they would include the newly elected supervisors.

Why does the Board of Supervisors need a lawyer anyway? There are plenty to consult with right under their feet. Is this another bill we taxpayers will have to pay? There is enough underhandedness in Washington, D.C. We do not need "anymore" of it here in the county. Enough already!

Chapter 9

2008

January 16, 2008

Driver Fees

I am all for fair "abusive driver" fees. The high fees are just what we need to wake some people up. It is evident that the little fines in place will not deter anyone. Something has to be done about the innocent people getting injured and killed on our highways by idiots that simply do not care.

So here is something that will surely work if anyone has the nerve to demand it. To put a stop to "abusive drivers" once and for all, put the first-time offenders in jail for six months, and add a stiff fine on top of that. It that doesn't work, try one to five years, depending on the offense. It is ok if the jails are overcrowded; they are there for the purpose of protecting "us" from "them." Make it illegal for them to own a car. If they get one from someone else, the person who gave it to them goes to jail too. It is time to stop scolding these stupid people and take serious action. How many more have to die before something is done? Change the law to include "all" drivers and it will be fair to everyone. It is the abusive drivers fault if money is taken from him or her that was needed for his family. No one else's. So put the blame where it belongs, on you.

Now I hear the Governor has repealed the abusive drivers law. Is this man totally insane? Leave it in place until all driver in the U.S are included, not just Virginians. And to those who scream it is not fair, listen up! Is it fair that all these innocent people are injured and killed because you chose to abuse the laws? Who do you think you are? It should be "one strike and you are out." You are not really living in a free country anymore. There are laws you have to obey when driving a vehicle and if you don't want to obey them, park the **** (damn) vehicle and walk.

Now, if the Governor thinks I am going to pay a higher sales tax, or any kind of tax to supplement what this fee would have brought in, think again. It is not fair to punish the decent drivers and taxpayers with higher fees for the abuses of drunks and reckless drivers. We pay and they continue to mame and kill. This is just another example of our lawmakers who refuse to use "common sense." Get them all out of office and elect your next-door neighbor. You will then see a change. "Common sense" wins every time.

March 8, 2008

Obama

With a few minutes to spare I will get in my two cents worth about the upcoming elections. After all the misery we have been through in the last eight years, why would any intelligent person vote for a Republican? That is a clear case of "cutting your own throat." One of the reasons being, there will never be an end to the war. And spare me the rhetoric about defending our country. They are only fighting for oil. We have no business in Iraq. They did not blow up the World Trade Center.

Our borders are being invaded, the economy is shot and we are trying to protect other countries when we can't even protect our own. How stupid is that? We have veterans lying in our streets that need taking care of. People need to stand up and get rid of the "idiots" in Congress. The power is with us. We are the ones who will have to end the war. We do need "change," but the Republicans in Congress will not work with Hillary. They do not like her. Remember Whitewater? So she is in no position to sling mud at Obama.

As a matter of fact, I would sleep just fine, if he wins. There is always the Cabinet (experts) to advise him, so enough already about the lack of experience. Tell me one thing good that "experience" has got us in the last eight years? So bring on Obama. I'm willing to give him four years. I'm not a wise old owl, but I have learned a few things over the past 67 years. The most important of which is to listen to your "senses." Think for yourself, people. "Don't believe nothing you hear and only half of what you see." Find out the history of the candidates yourself and then vote. Know whom you are voting for. Become an Independent, because then you will not follow your party down the road of no return. A die-hard Republican or Democrat will follow their party no matter how corrupt. That is dangerous for everyone. Vote for what the person stands for and not the party. You had better get it right this time around because we don't have much time left.

May 15, 2008

Gays

I have finally graduated from college after 12 long years, so it's back to letter writing. There seems to be some people upset with California's decision to lift the ban on gay marriage. What gives some people the right to dictate to others how to live? Everyone is created equal, or should be, and they are free to live as they see fit. People should remember if God does not like it, he will handle it in his own way in due time. That should give those who are worried some comfort. Many cannot control their own lives, much less someone else's. So people should live their own lives and leave others alone.

I attended church from infants to young people, but I do not go now because of the way many churches put people down in the name of God. I went to church to be taught from the Bible and not someone's personal opinion. Not everyone interprets the Bible the same. I can talk to God right here at home, thank you very much, and I don't have to rub shoulders with hypocrites who go to church just to be seen, and go back to stabbing people in the back the minute church is over. And believe me, I know some. There are some among the faithful. It's not the gays who will hasten Gods return; it's the people and their treatment of each other.

Moving on, what's up with McCain? Regardless of what party you are in, this thing about staying in Iraq until 2013 is absurd. How many kids does he think there are in the U.S. that are still alive and able to serve? Where is he going to get them from? Those left sure aren't going to enlist and sign their death warrant, unless they are brainwashed. We are not in Iraq to defend this country. Now, if they come over here, that's a whole different ballgame. Five more years of being involved in a war that we can never win will wipe out every young man in this country. So if it happens, the old folks had better bone up on their survival skills, because they will be serving next.

The only way this country will be able to survive is to keep our money here and take care of our own. The economy is not going to improve the way it is going now. Better hope things change after the election or we are all done for.

May 23, 2008

Law Enforcement

A few thought's concerning those in law enforcement who put their life on the line everyday to protect us. I believe some people have no idea or care about how dangerous a job law enforcement is. The problem we have is they are not paid nearly enough money. To hire the very best people you have to pay them a decent salary. Would you put your life on the line for the "chicken scratch" they make? Top-notch people and enough of them would make a big difference in crime. And, the county can find enough money.

Another thing this county needs are speed cameras. They will free up the deputies and produce enough money to pay for them ten times over. More important, they could lower taxes with the money they produce. And for those who scream about their privacy being violated, there is this. You have no privacy in public. Behave yourself and don't do things you do not want known, or face the consequences.

Try complaining about something important for a change. Some people are so worried about their "rights" they lose sight of a bigger problem. Get out and scream about the crooks in Congress who take money from special interest, sell their souls to the devil and all the "pork" they waste our tax dollars on. They are the important things to complain about. Demand they pass laws to put an end to both or vote them out of office. People have the power to do it and they are the only ones who can. But it seems they want to just sit and complain.

May 28, 2008

War

I have been hearing our veterans want their college education they were promised when they enlisted. But the President is going to veto the bill that was recently passed. The cost of their four years of college would be $2 billion dollars. It has been said to cost too much. But, that is absurd. The war in Iraq is costing us $2 billion a month! One month! Now, ain't them some apples?

As for the Iraq fiasco, McCain says he will never surrender. Well, I wonder how much that has to do with him having been a POW? When you have a "tortured" veteran, a war could become very personal. To me, that is disturbing. He will never end the war if the terrorists never give up, so we will be over there forever, unless we just leave. The heck with saving "face." We do not have any "face" left to save.

We have no right to push our ways on other countries. The terrorists are raising their children up to be martyrs. As fast as one dies, there are ten to take their place. They have been fighting since the beginning of time and they will be fighting until the end of time. So, you tell me how we are ever going to end the war, other than just leaving? We won't drop the bomb because it will kill to many innocent people, and the terrorists know it. They have their own beliefs, which should be evident by now. No one can win, so bring our troops and money home. We cannot save the whole world. The other countries know it and that is why they had the good sense to stay out of it. Some things you just have to leave to God to take care of.

We need people with "plain ole common sense" to run the military and not be puppets to the "quacks" we have in Washington right now. Washington knows what kind of people they are dealing with, but are brainwashing people into believing the war can be won. I say again, the terrorist will fight forever. They will never quit.

There is "pride" and then there is "stupidity." Which one is this country sporting right now? They had better come down off that "high horse" before they get us all killed. Take care of our own for once! Think of what $2 billion a month could get us.

June 11, 2008

School Board

Would those on the Board of Supervisors who think there would be to many problems to allow the taxpayers to elect the School Board members, (or any other official), please explain what they are. Us dumb taxpayers would like to know. If you can't come up with any, put their names on the ballot, and let the taxpayers elect them.

We the people should elect everyone. It is our county and our tax dollars. So explain! We are owed at least that much. There are enough closed-door meeting's, cover-ups and appointments in Washington, D.C. See the problems they have caused? They have been quietly hidden here in the county for years and people are getting tired of it. The county officials should rise up above this.

The Code of Virginia, §2.2–3711. A.1, (the excuse to hold closed-door meetings) states "Discussion or consideration of the assignment, appointment, promotion, performance, demotion, salaries, disciplining or resignation of specific public offices, appointees, or employees of any public body." What part of the these does the taxpayers not have a right to know, being we pay their salaries and they answer to us? Public servants put themselves out there when they accept the office. Good or bad, we have the right to know what they say and what they do. That is the only way to keep them honest. Can you think of a better way to keep our officials above board?

Enough already with the closed-door meetings. Turn the "appointments" over to the taxpayers where they belong and open those doors to those who own them!

July 10, 2008

Roads

I find it amusing how the Democrats and Republicans always vote party lines. That is why they can never get anything done. What are the Republicans trying to do to our roads? They are cutting everyone's throat, including their own with their recent decision not to provide road funding.

Now, the reason I find it amusing is that in a way it would be the answer to some of our prayers, in regard to speeders. Since there will not be enough money to keep up the roads, we will have to dodge potholes, even on the bypasses. That could be the answer to this problem of nuts not knowing the difference between the gas pedal and the brake. It sure would cut down on speeding by most.

Personally, I think when the roads get bad enough they should be replaced with 'good ole gravel'. Can you think of a better way to control speeders? They would not dare fly down gravel roads and sling gravel up on their nice expensive vehicles, chipping paint and filling them full of dents. And, those brakes will not do them any good either, because there will be no asphalt or concrete to grab on to. Many will just slide on over a cliff or into a tree. Maybe that will slow them down. They do not pay any attention to a ticket because they aren't worth the money they are printed on. Since the government will not hit them hard in the pocketbook, let's go back to gravel. It just may save lives, conserve fuel, free up the Sheriff's Department to concentrate on violent crimes, and cut cost too. You can bet with response times cut by the fire department and rescue squads, people will be more careful. People have to have some responsibility for their actions. Any better ideas?

Another thing that needs addressing is the spraying to kill vegetation on Izaak Walton Road. AEP, Verizon, or whoever should clean up that blight, trees standing up and down the road, dead. Don't be so lazy, just walk through there and cut them down. It sure is an eyesore and most of our citizens do not want to look at this destruction of nature. We pay enough on our utility bills to take care of it.

July 18, 2008

House

Some comments on real estate appraisals. Why does the county allow someone to appraise just the outside of houses? The outside is only part of the appraisal. I heard of a house that has been appraised for way over its value, but the inside has been trashed, so to speak. You cannot take a house and appraise it "way over its value" in that condition. That should be considered stealing. The county needs to have someone check the inside of unoccupied houses that are "on the market" to see if they are still worth the appraisal. They should re-access if necessary to be fair. The county should readjust the value.

Today houses aren't worth much, just the lot it sits on. So why appraise the house way over it's value? No one minds paying a fair price, but people do not like being taken advantage of. Banks are no better. Many are so greedy, they could care less what the house is "really" like, and they just take the appraisers word. And you wonder why so many are failing.

There needs to be some type of legislation passed to protect the taxpayers from paying too much for real estate that is not worth it. With the housing market in shambles, appraisals should be fair and those who disagree with an appraisal should be given the opportunity to prove the price is out of line, anytime, not just when appraisals are done. Use your head Amherst. Let people here decide the value of "our" properties, not someone out of never, never land. As it is now, people are being taken advantage of and it should not be allowed. But, I guess as P.T. Barnum says, "there is a sucker born every minute," but I wouldn't be one of them.

July 25, 2008

Complaints

We have a serious problem with many who are employed in Amherst, and it's time for it to be addressed. Most are not taxpayer friendly. You can call or email and no reply ever comes, with the exception of the Sheriff's Department, one nice lady at the Board of Equalization and Mr. Adams of the Board of Supervisors. Since we pay their salaries, they should be eager to get back to us quickly. They are not serving the citizens of Amherst County, with the exception of "their" friends. The rest of us are left out in the cold.

When you go out there, have you ever noticed how many look at you as if you are their worst nightmare? I can understand that if they know who I am, but most don't and they still give you that glare. It is time for the department heads (and some under them) to be "people friendly" and serve the people like they do each other. If not, they need to be replaced. A word of advice, take time to be useful and friendly towards your "employers," and that would be the taxpayer's. The elections are looming.

We need people out there that make you feel welcome and will bend over backwards to help you. That has not been done, so enough of the "good ole boy" mentality. If I worked out here, you would see a big difference, because I would be very aware of who was paying my salary. I would treat those I served with respect, and all the help they could ever want. I would fine answers for them and not just leave them stranded. Where have all the good public servants gone? They sure aren't in Amherst.

This letter did not go over well, but if the shoe fits, wear it.

August 17, 2008

Little League

The start of Little League football is upon us once again and as usual, problems. Some changes need to be made in how they manage the kids that do not make the team and it is long overdue. Do they have any idea as to how cutting them after tryouts really affects them? I don't think they care. It is all about winning at any cost. It is a sport people, and as such should be more about teamwork and building character in the kids. Winning should be looked at as a "reward" and not as something you must do at any cost. It is not a life and death situation.

If you have a large child, use them in an offensive tackle position, etc. instead of a position that requires a lot of speed. You do not make excused for cutting them by saying they did not get their physical on time, when one child's was obtained the second day of tryouts, or using some other lame excuse not to make them part of the team. They need to boost these kids confidence and let them know they can do anything they set their mind to, but a little help might be needed. Create practice sessions for those who do not make the team and groom them for next year. Take them to all the games as a member of a future team. They can learn a lot by watching. Do not just toss them aside.

This is no different than tossing them out like the garbage. Sorry, you're no good, out with the trash. Think about these kids for a change and their feelings, our future leaders, and not the almighty glory of an upcoming win. Put a program into place to build these kids up, not tear them down. It is time to do something for the kids who have had their dreams shattered. They are just as important as those who make the team. The county should be ashamed, heck, all of Little League should be.

August 27, 2008

Get the Facts

This letter is in response to the Aug. 21 letter to the editor written by Wendy Nash regarding "little league" football.

In reading the letter, one thing became very apparent. She is not familiar with the youth football programs. They do not cut any child from their teams. Our coaches and board members are all volunteers and take great pride in coaching and teaching the children in our program.

The unfortunate part of this letter and the paper's decision to print it is that the readers who may not know the truth about our program may get the wrong impression about our organization.

In the future, please do not write or print derogatory letters about volunteer youth organizations until you have all the facts.

Karl Tatlock
President, Amherst Wolverines Football and Cheerleading

August 27, 2008

Reply to Little League Coach

In response to the letter from Mr. Tatlock, I would like to clear up a few of its misconceptions. I stand by the "fact" at least two kids were in tears over not "playing" with the team, and I am "familiar" with the football program as my son played some 15 years ago. Things have changed some, but not the reaction of the kids that couldn't "play" on the team.

I think it would be a good idea to enlighten the readers as to what the "truth"/ "facts" are about the program. What happens to the kids that do not get to play? Do they get to practice for next year, as well as being water boys?

My letter was not about what I do or do not know about "little league" football, but about some of the kids and their disappointments. And, don't worry about people getting the wrong idea about your organization. Just give us the "facts" about what happens to the kids that do not "play" and everything will smooth out.

And, I agree the coaches, volunteers and board members are proud of what they do and we need more of them.

Last, but not least, lay off of the newspapers. We need a free press, where "everyone" can give their opinion. When we lose that right, we are in trouble. It is hard to find newspapers these days with the guts to print issues that stir debate, as many are controlled by their local government. We should all thank God we still have a few around.

August 30. 2008

L. U.

The Liberty University/ Obama parking problem could have been solved quite simply. First, you should have agreed to let them use the parking lot with the understanding they would be billed. And turn around, and donate the money back to the Obama campaign. That would have been "being a good neighbor." Problem solved. It's not like Liberty needed the money. Obama doesn't either, but it would have been the Christian thing to do. I am sure the Obama students on campus would have approved.

The most important question here is, "What would God have done?" I don't think he would have charged the public $10.00 for a parking spot!

The *Lynchburg News and Advance* would not publish this letter.

September 17, 2008

Morals

Evangelical voters view abortion as morally wrong. But, to me, allowing the killing of any innocent soul is just as immoral, and is also looked down upon by God. If evangelicals cannot live with abortion, how can they live with the fact this government, which they partly control, is allowing the killing of all the people in Iraq and Afghanistan, in so called "wars" that can never be won? I do not hear any uproar from them over their deaths? If we protect a fetus, we should protect our people who serve in the military. Let them serve and protect right here at home. If we allow the "wars" to continue, we are just as guilty as those who are doing the killing. Our servicemen enlist to protect our country, but that is not who they are protecting. People need to do some soul searching and ask themselves why our servicemen and women are not just as important as a fetus and do something about it.

How can anyone vote for a candidate who plans to continue "wars" that can never be won, knowing full well we can never stop the violence over there? If the Republicans win, thousands more will die. Make no mistake about that. We are going to see a "real" surge when the enemy regroups and we won't be the ones that will be doing the winning. But, this government already knows that.

Our lives are also at stake here. Everyone knows what Bin Laden did when we would not leave Afghanistan after we started meddling over there. We were warned then. And, we are still over there looking for mountain rats we will never find. If we stay there, the terrorist will hit us again. It is just a matter of time. And the next time it will be far worse. The present administration won't even talk to them. How stupid is that? I pass on to them this phase worth remembering, "Keep you friends close and your enemies closer." Our lives may depend on it.

We cannot save the world, but we can save ourselves, and all of those innocent souls fighting for nothing. Get out of the Middle East. It is not our country. Think about it come election time, and ask yourself if who you vote for is worth all those peoples lives that will continue to be lost. This moral issue is just as important as abortion. The question is: what are the evangelical's and other voters going to do about it?

October 15, 2008

Obama Sign

This letter is to the person who stole an Obama sign from my driveway on Izaak Walton Road. I have given it a lot of thought and I want to thank you. There is nothing like a sign thief to inspire me to do my best work. It so inspired me that I found eight new Obama voters, so far. And just think, through your actions you are contributing to his being elected and many of us couldn't be more pleased.

So I hope everyone who has a sign stolen goes out and finds many more voters. It is so reassuring to know there are so many out there who are helping him win the election. Thanks again for all those new votes for Obama. I'm sure there will be many more to come.

And, if it is not returned, I will find another sign and put it up. But the next time you attempt to steal it, beware! It will be hooked up to a little juice. And if you grab hold of it, you will light up like a Christmas tree. It's a little early to celebrate Christmas, but I'm game if you are.

The Amherst New-Era Progress **did not publish this letter. Gee, I was only giving people notice.**

October 27, 2008

Economy

The answer to fixing our economy is simple. Our government, "we the people" should make the financial institutions and Wall Street pay back our money, if they have to sell everything they own. Just like the rest of us would have to do. And, then put them in jail. It should be done now. Then you would see a confidence in the people that would get us back on track and right now, not years down the road. Justice would be served and our economy would soar.

You want confidence? Make them pay now. That would do more for the country than any bailout. If Congress does not go along, elect a new one, with rules. No special interest, frills and lobbyists, etc. or walk the unemployment line. Congress is allowing our money to be wiped out. Get rid of most of them. This country will not prosper with the majority of the ones we have in there now. Enough is enough! You want a simple fix to the economy? This is it!

November 29, 2008

Congress

With the elections over it is time to make some more changes. The oil companies got our message and now it is time to take on Congress. With the way they are wasting out tax dollars, we need to step in and demand a stop to the handouts to those greedy CEO's. If they won't, there is one surefire way to stop them. We refuse to pay any more taxes! What are they going to do? There are not enough jails to hold us all. They are already filled, so there is no room for us "victims." And with no money for salaries, do they think law enforcement will work for nothing?

If they do find a place to stuff us, we will have to be fed and then we can lie around and watch TV all day. We can write letters from our cell and cook with the trustees. Doesn't sound so bad to me.

Or, we could just quit our jobs. Live off the government like many already do. That is what welfare is for. There will be no one to sell our houses to if we are all in jail or detained somewhere, so there will be no money for them there.

As for food, they may have to push down some of those developments they allowed to be built on that precious farmland, and turn them back into farms. We are playing Russian roulette buying imported food.

If we can send a man to the moon, build a space station, perfect DNA, and cure diseases, surely we can figure out a way to put people in office that do not fight like Banny roosters and will lookout for our money and not themselves. But, that's Congress for yah, and it's time to put a stop to their waste.

December 3, 2008

Deer Hunters

On the news this past week there was a group who went deer hunting and they were shown with two deer they had killed. One was just a baby deer. Many have a problem with anyone killing a baby deer. Hunting is all well and good if you need food, but there is no meat on them, so I guess that was for sport? How do you justify killing a defenseless baby deer and calling it a sport?

If there is an "over population," it's the fault of human. We have taken away their habitat, so where do you think they will go for food if not to people's yards? God put plants on this earth for the wildlife as well as man. God said nothing about yards being off-limits. And they need to cross the roads to get to them, so, slow down and be aware or pay the price.

Now for those who say they have the "right" to kill them because the law says so, think about this. There are plenty of stupid laws on the books. Animals were put here on the earth for food, not sport. That is man's stupid idea. God would not approve of killing them for any other reason. There is a life cycle to take care of so-called "overpopulation."

Why don't we just have open season of us humans? No one is controlling our population. That would level the playing field, don't you think?

Some deer hunters are also leaving deer carcasses in the woods. That can cause exposure to infections, such as, salmonella, e-coli and other pathogens and spread disease to the general public and the wildlife population. Pass a law about that.

And, one last big question that no one seems to know the answer too. What does anyone get from hanging an animal's head on the wall and bragging about it? Is it some kind of macho thing? Do they think it makes them a bigger man or woman? Well, I've got news for yah, it doesn't. The real measure of a man or woman is how they treat those around them, both animals and people. Remember, what goes around, comes around. That's a given.

Of course, I never got a response.

December 28, 2008

Obama

As we start a new year, this country is heading upward. I have never been one to believe much in intuition, but now that has all changed. I saw Obama four years ago at the 2004 Democratic Convention and predicted he would be the first black President of the United States and that prediction was right on the money.

I can't explain it, but he is magic. When he speaks, it is riveting. In all my years I have never seen anyone like him. Many countries agree, as was evident when he visited overseas this past summer. You cannot fool the whole world. He is a true gift.

There is no question he will do what he says he can do. He will change this country and it will be much sooner than most expect. He will bring leaders together and solve problems wars can never do. Just watch and see.

We all need to support him. He will need our help. We now have the chance to have a say in forming the new America. Take advantage of it. If not for us, then do it for our grandchildren and future generations. No more sitting around complaining. If you want change, you have to become involved. Check out: www.change.gov and speak your mind, and thank God for Barack Obama. Change has arrived and not a moment to soon. Go Obama!

Final Thoughts

People need to stand up and speak out now. It took me 60 + years to realize how we were losing our rights and time was running out on the ones we had left. So, as a result, this book was written. I hope it inspires others to get involved in what is going on around them and not wait sixty years to do so. By then, it may be too late. My Letters to the Editor will continue as long as I am alive. Standing up and speaking out is our only hope, so "Go, People."

As of 2008, the dump road is fixed for the present, Izaak Walton finally got paved, the stop light was put up, the developers have been put in their place for the present by the recession, we have 2 new supervisors, but things are still "rocky" in Amherst. What will it take to find officials that represent the people, and not money and influence?

We still have no art gallery, no speed cameras, "pot" is still illegal and tobacco and alcohol are still legal, so I guess there is more work to be done. But the one saving grace is this, **"I am still alive and kicking"** and watching the county officials. And, those folks had better keep on their toes, because I am going nowhere.

…..to be continued. The best is yet to come!

Printed in the United States
by Baker & Taylor Publisher Services